The Essex Police Force

A History

The Armorial Bearings of
ESSEX POLICE
as Recorded in Her Majesty's College of Arms

Conrad Swan
12.VIII.93 Garter

Garter Principal King of Arms

BRITAIN IN OLD PHOTOGRAPHS

THE ESSEX POLICE FORCE A HISTORY

MARTYN LOCKWOOD

First published 2009

The History Press
The Mill, Brimscombe Port
Stroud, Gloucestershire, GL5 2QG
www.thehistorypress.co.uk

British Library Cataloguing in Publication Data.
A catalogue record for this book is available from the British Library.

ISBN 978 0 7524 5167 1

Typesetting and origination by The History Press
Printed in Great Britain

CONTENTS

	Acknowledgements and Author's Note	6
	Introduction	7
1.	Essex County Constabulary, 1840–1969	9
2.	Colchester Borough Constabulary, 1836-1947	71
3.	Southend Borough Constabulary, 1914-1969	85
4.	Essex and Southend-on-Sea Joint Constabulary, 1969-1974	107
5.	Essex Police, 1974 to the Present Day	115

ACKNOWLEDGEMENTS

The author would particularly like to thank the Chief Constable, Mr Roger Baker; the Essex Police Authority; and the Trustees of the Essex Police Museum for allowing the use of photographs from their collection.

There are many other people who have contributed in some way to the preparation of this book, including Becky Wash, the full-time curator of Essex Police Museum, who has allowed me free rein with the material in the museum. I am also indebted to Alan Cook, Brian Turner, Fred Feather and many others who have loaned photographs, shared memories and, mostly importantly, given their expert advice. I am also indebted to the Essex Police Photographic Department for reproducing many of the illustrations used in this book.

Finally, I should mention three books on the history of policing in Essex all written by serving officers: John Woodgate's *The Essex Police*, published in 1985; Maureen Scollan's *Sworn to Serve*, published in 1993; and Inspector Bert Williams and PC Peter Doxsey's *A Brief History of the Southend on Sea County Borough Constabulary on the Occasion of its Golden Jubilee 1914-1964*. I can recommend all three books to those who would like to know more about the history of policing in the county.

I believe that I have obtained permissions to use the photographs where necessary, or have used those which are out of copyright. If I have breached any copyright, my apologies.

AUTHOR'S NOTE

The Essex Police Museum was opened in 1991 and was the inspiration of two men: Peter Simpson OBE, former Deputy Chief Constable of Essex from 1986 until his retirement in 1993; and Tony Peel, son of former Chief Constable, Sir Jonathan Peel, sometime Chair of the Essex Police Authority and Chair of Essex County Council and a friend to many in the police service. Peter was Chair of the Trustees for many years. Sadly both men have passed away, Tony in July 2008, and Peter in September 2008; they will be greatly missed. This book is dedicated to their memory.

Royalties from this book will go towards the continued support of the Essex Police Museum, and the upkeep of the collection. The museum, which is a registered charity, is open to the public and details of opening times can be obtained by visiting the website, www.essex.police.uk/museum

INTRODUCTION

In 1840 Essex was one of the first counties to establish a police force under the provisions of the County Police Act 1839. Resistance to the establishment of police forces in the country was founded on a number of deep-rooted fears: the traditional misgivings of a standing army; the political uses which might be made of such a force; the effects of police intrusion upon daily neighbourhood life; and the fear that they would be used to enforce the new Poor Law. Middle-class people often objected out of rate consciousness, while those living in rural areas could see a need for policing in cities, but felt the expense of keeping them in the countryside far outweighed their potential usefulness (the cost of the Essex Constabulary in 1840 amounted to £9,300).

While Essex took early advantage under the 1839 Act to establish a professional police force, the provisions of the Municipal Corporations Act of 1835 allowed for the creation of chartered boroughs and included a requirement to form a Watch Committee, and within three weeks of their appointment to employ constables to preserve the peace within the borough. As a result Colchester, Saffron Walden, Harwich and Maldon formed their own police forces. Maldon's was formed in January 1836 and initially employed eleven men. By the time of its amalgamation with Essex, on 1 April 1889, it only had five constables. Harwich was also formed in January 1836 and initially employed twelve constables. The force was abolished in February 1857, and at this time employed only five constables. Saffron Walden also formed a police force but its records are scarce and it was, like Harwich, abolished on 1 November 1857. The strength of the force is unknown, although its chief officer, William Campling, was murdered in 1849, a crime for which no one was convicted. Colchester fared best; formed on 28 February 1836, it was to remain a separate force until 1 April 1947, when it was amalgamated with Essex. With an initial strength of twenty men, by 1947 it had risen to seventy-seven. Colchester recruited many of its officers from the local military garrison.

The Essex County Constabulary came into existence on 1 April 1840. Initially a hundred constables and fifteen Superintendents were appointed. Thirty-one applicants applied for the position of Chief Constable, and, after interviewing nineteen of them, the magistrates appointed Captain McHardy, a former naval officer, at a salary of £400 per year.

From the outset McHardy had to contend with widespread distrust shown to the force, but gradually he won the support of the magistracy and the local communities. In many respects his contribution to the establishment of county police forces throughout the country was comparable to that of Rowan and Mayne in the establishment and development of the Metropolitan Police from 1829.

In 1914 Southend Corporation demanded the right to have its own police force and this was achieved on 1 April 1914, when Southend was granted county borough status. The first Chief Constable was Henry Maurice Kerslake, who came from Dewsbury in West Yorkshire. He was allowed to select 101 officers to make up the new force.

Essex Constabulary officers, who were already policing the town, were given the option of remaining in Essex or transferring to the new force. Seventy-three officers chose to transfer and of these thirteen were promoted.

With the introduction of the 1964 Police Act, the Home Secretary was given powers to make compulsory amalgamations and many smaller borough forces disappeared. Southend, however, was able to remain a separate force until 1 April 1969, when, following a public enquiry, it was amalgamated with Essex. The new force, under the command of John Nightingale, the Chief Constable of Essex, became known as the Essex and Southend-on-Sea Joint Constabulary. However, this name was short-lived and in 1974, with the introduction of the Local Government Act, which reformed local government and gave one police force per county, the force was renamed the Essex Police.

From those early beginnings in 1840, Essex Police today employs 3,500 police officers and 2,200 support staff (2009 figures). Hopefully this book will show some of the changes that have occurred over the past 170 years.

Martyn Lockwood, 2009

ONE

ESSEX COUNTY CONSTABULARY 1840–1969

Above left: John Bunch Bonnemaison McHardy (1801-1883) was appointed Chief Constable of Essex County Constabulary by the Justices on 11 February 1840. Although only thirty-eight years old, McHardy already had a long career in the Royal Navy and the coastguard behind him, having joined the navy at the age of eleven from his home in the British-owned Bahamas. After retiring from the navy as a captain on half pay, McHardy was chosen from thirty-one candidates for the post of Chief Constable, a position he was to hold for the next forty-one years, retiring at the age of eighty, in October 1881. He had remained on the active list of officers in the navy and, being eligible for promotion, eventually attained the rank of Admiral in 1870. He often signed documents with this rank. McHardy died at the home of his daughter in Bath on 3 October 1883 and was buried in the family tomb in Holy Trinity Church, Springfield, Chelmsford. *(Essex Police Museum)*

Above right: Initially a hundred constables and fifteen Superintendents were appointed to the constabulary. Constables were provided with a basic uniform of a blue dress coat with embroidered collar, dress trousers, 'undress' trousers, waterproofed greatcoat, cape, pair of boots, pair of shoes and a black stove pipe hat. It was not until the 1870s that the familiar helmet was adopted. Anyone who resigned had to pay 5*s* to have the uniform altered for the next recruit. Constables were also issued with a rattle, truncheon and a pair of handcuffs, and were required to supply themselves with two pairs of white drill trousers, which were to be worn 'whenever the Superintendent may direct, between 1 May and 1 October'. The style of uniform changed over the century, the dress coat being replaced by the frock coat, as seen in this photograph of Walter Newell from 1871 *(Essex Police Museum)*

No. 142.

ORDERS AND INSTRUCTIONS

FRAMED AND ISSUED

FOR THE GOVERNMENT

OF THE

ESSEX COUNTY CONSTABULARY,

Under the Act 2 & 3 Vict. cap. 93,
And the authority of the Marquis of Normanby, one of Her Majesty's principal Secretaries of State:

APPROVED BY

THE JUSTICES IN QUARTER SESSION,

On the 3rd day of July, 1849.

BY

J. B. B. Mc HARDY, Capt. Royal Navy,

AND

Chief Constable of Essex.

CHELMSFORD:

PRINTED BY J. SHEARCROFT.

Far left: The earliest known photograph of an Essex officer shows Inspector John Harris Bausor, a native of Nottinghamshire and former seaman, who was born in 1811. He joined Essex in 1841 as Constable No. 5. He was promoted to Inspector in 1844 and died in post in 1861. The uniform pictured here is that of an Inspector. It consisted of a blue cloth double-breasted coat with a half-inch black braid around the collar. *(Essex Police Museum)*

Left: By the end of 1840 the strength of the force stood at seventeen Superintendents, eighteen Inspectors and sixty-seven constables. Captain McHardy issued a booklet in 1849 to all officers, containing 'Orders and Instructions for the Government of the Essex County Constabulary'. *(Essex Police Museum)*

50

leave of absence; and they are to report themselves at the Chief Constable's office, whenever in its neighbourhood.

Sect. 6. Limit attendance of Constables at Sessions.

To avoid the attendance of more constables than are indispensably necessary at Sessions, Superintendents will select a constable located at their respective head quarters, for the purpose of, as far as practicable, serving all summonses: and will exercise every means in their power, to limit the assemblage or detention of Constables at Sessions.

Sect. 7. Superintendents to accompany accused.

Whenever a charge is taken before a Magistrate by any one under the Superintendents orders, the Superintendent must invariably accompany the accused, for the purpose of answering any questions the Magistrates may think proper to ask.

Sect. 8. Superintendents to report on Reports forwarded to the Chief Constable.

Superintendents are always to report their own opinion fully, on all applications, reports, or other documents forwarded by them to the Chief Constable; taking care previously, to make strict enquiries, when necessary.

Sect. 9. Superintendents to report improper connection and suggest removals and alterations.

The Superintendent is to report to the Chief Constable, any improper connections formed by those under his command, or any deficiency of strength, courage, or activity; and to suggest for his consideration, any removals or alterations which may from time to time appear to him necessary, either in his company, or otherwise; noting the same in the journal.

51

Sect. 10. To keep order book.

Superintendents are to keep the General Order Books, which are furnished for their Divisions, and copy in them all such written orders, as may be issued from time to time by the Chief Constable, and index the same; and they are to attach their signatures to all documents which may be forwarded for their information, prior to their being returned to the Chief Constable. The dates upon which the said documents may have been received, and copied, are also to be noted.

Sect. 11. Repairs and Stores.

When repairs, stores, or arms of any description are required, Superintendents are to deliver to the Chief Constable a statement thereof, in sufficient time to have the same duly provided; and when the application refers to repairs, or stores to be supplied on the spot, Superintendents will attach estimates, in duplicate, from at least two respectable tradesmen, for executing the necessary repairs, or supplying the required stores.

Sect. 12. Constables to be numbered.

The constables are to be numbered from one upwards, and when there is occasion to mention in the journal occurrences relating to any individual, the No. is to be used instead of the name, and letters in like manner for inspectors.

Sect. 13. Correspondence with Chief Constable.

Superintendents in corresponding with the Chief Constable, are to number their letters, commencing with No. 1. on the first letter of each year.

All letters are to be written on foolscap paper, with

Pages from the booklet giving instructions as to the role of the Superintendent. *(Essex Police Museum)*

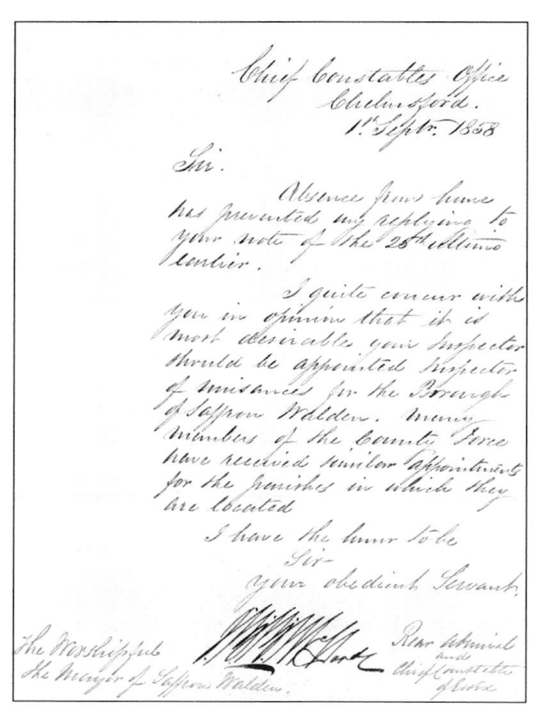

Chief Constables Office
Chelmsford.
1st Septr. 1858

Sir.

Absence from home has prevented my replying to your note of the 25th Ultimo earlier.

I quite concur with you in opinion that it is most desirable your Inspector should be appointed Inspector of nuisances for the Borough of Saffron Walden. Many members of the County Force have received similar appointments for the parishes in which they are located.

I have the honor to be
Sir
your obedient Servant

W W McHardy
Rear Admiral and Chief Constable of Essex

The Worshipful the Mayor of Saffron Walden.

This letter, dated 1 September 1858, from McHardy to the Mayor of Saffron Walden, reads:

'Absence from home has prevented my replying to your note of the 25th ultimo earlier. I quite concur with you in opinion that it is most desirable your Inspector should be appointed Inspector of Nuisances for the Borough of Saffron Walden. Many members of the County Force have received similar appointments for the parishes in which they are located.'

The letter is signed by McHardy, who refers to himself as 'Rear Admiral and Chief Constable.' It was usual within Essex for Superintendents and Inspectors to be given a variety of other duties, including Inspectors of weights and measures and Inspectors under the Poor Law Act of 1834. *(Essex Police Museum)*

PC 221 James Ballard, who joined the constabulary in 1867 and retired in 1891. Note the bowler hat he is wearing, which was in service during McHardy's time as Chief Constable. Constables worked long hours, often under difficult conditions; the average working day was between ten and twelve hours, split into two shifts. A day shift of three or four hours was followed by a night shift between 10 p.m. and dawn. This was performed seven days a week – a rest day not being granted until 1914. Even then, a constable was still not allowed to leave his station without permission. *(Essex Police Museum)*

Left: There was obviously still time for recreation however, as our photograph of James Ballard with his wife and eleven children shows. Often a village constable's wife was expected to answer queries and take message for her husband, for which she would receive no remuneration. *(Essex Police Museum)*

Below: William Barnard, who joined the constabulary in November 1872. The photograph shows him in the uniform of a constable, wearing the top hat of the period. Barnard rose to the rank of Superintendent, dying in service in 1909. *(Essex Police Museum)*

Right: In 1875 the now familiar helmet was introduced, as shown here with Acting Sergeant Charles Wood, taken when he was stationed at Matching. He joined the force in 1876, retiring in 1906. The rank of Sergeant was not introduced into the force until 1854, and it was usual for officers to be promoted to the rank of Acting Sergeant before reaching the substantive rank. *(Essex Police Museum)*

Far right: Victorian helmet plate displaying the seaxes shield in the centre. *(Essex Police Museum)*

Above: The Merit Star, or Merit Badge as it is sometimes referred to, was the initiative of McHardy and was introduced into Essex in June 1871. It was to be awarded to officers for 'highly distinguished and discreet conduct in the discharge of their duty particularly when accompanied with risk of life personal courage and coolness, aided by marked intelligence'. The first constable to receive the Merit Star was PC John Street of Foxearth in the Hinckford Division, on 17 January 1872, who was violently assaulted when he arrested three men for theft. *(Essex Police Museum)*

Above: Sergeant Richard Giggins wearing the Merit Badge on his right sleeve. It was awarded to him in 1895 for 'meritorious conduct in a case of corn stealing'. The badge on his left arm is that of the St John Ambulance, awarded to officers who passed an examination in first-aid. Giggins is also wearing his whistle, which were introduced in 1889 to replace rattles. It cost £16 4*s* to equip the whole force at this time. *(Essex Police Museum)*

Left: Superintendent David Scott in his parade uniform. Next to the crown on his collar he wears the Merit Star, which was awarded to him in 1899 for 'the intelligence he showed in a case of murder'. David Scott served in Essex from 1883 until his retirement in 1920. As a Detective Sergeant he was involved in the investigation into the disappearance of Camille Holland, who had been murdered by Samuel Herbert Dougal at Moat Farm, Clavering in 1899. Scott was one of the officers who discovered the body. Dougal was convicted of the crime and was hanged at Chelmsford Prison in 1903. *(Essex Police Museum)*

Left: Superintendent William Creasey (1874-1905), wearing the 'kepi' style hat worn by senior officers. Although he retired in 1905, he again offered his services to the police during the First World War and for the duration held the rank of Inspector and was in charge of the special constables in the Tendring area. *(Essex Police Museum)*

Below: Superintendent George William Terry joined in 1873. A former groom, he served at Chelmsford, Mistley, Thorpe and Braintree. He was promoted to Superintendent in 1898 and placed in charge of the Braintree Division. He retired from the force in 1913. *(Essex Police Museum)*

Above left: The first purpose-built police station in Essex was constructed at Dunmow and opened in 1843 and was in regular use until it was replaced by a new building in 2008. The cost of the original station was £1,100, which included cells and stables. *(Essex Police Museum)*

Above right: Saffron Walden police station was built in 1884 to replace Newport Gaol and is still in use today. *(Essex Police Museum)*

Above: A group of officers stationed at Witham in 1876. In the following year Acting Sergeants no longer wore the crown above their chevrons. Police officers were also allowed to vote in parliamentary elections for the first time.

Left: A group of officers stationed at Southminster, *c.* 1893. *(Essex Police Museum)*

William Henry Poyntz succeed McHardy as Chief Constable on 1 November 1881. He was born in Dublin in 1838 and commissioned into the Royal Marine Light Infantry in October 1853, serving in Hong Kong, China, Japan and at home in Woolwich. He was appointed Chief Constable of Nottingham in 1871 before coming to Essex. Major Poyntz was a keen disciplinarian and he dealt severely with those who drank on duty. He retired through ill health in July 1887. His autobiography, *Per Mare, Per Terram*, was published just before his death in 1892. The title of the book came from the motto of the Royal Marines, which means, By Sea, By Land. *(Essex Police Museum)*

Sergeant John Harvey served in the West Riding of Yorkshire before transferring to Essex in 1885. He was posted to Ardleigh on 6 January 1886 and promoted to Sergeant there on 1 October 1891. On 4 January 1894 John Harvey disappeared whilst on duty. He was last seen by his fellow constables at about 7.30 p.m. The following morning his body was found head first down a well in the snow-covered garden of a cottage in Ardleigh; his watch had stopped at 8.21 p.m. There were injuries to the face, but it could not be determined with certainty how they had been caused. It has never been proved whether the Sergeant fell or if he was pushed. He had a wife and three children, with a fourth on the way. *(Essex Police Museum)*

ORDERS AND INSTRUCTIONS

FOR THE GUIDANCE OF THE

ESSEX CONSTABULARY

ISSUED BY

MAJOR W. H. POYNTZ,

Chief Constable of the County.

WITH THE APPROVAL OF THE JUSTICES IN QUARTER SESSION ASSEMBLED.

EASTER SESSION, 1882.

CHELMSFORD:
PRINTED AT THE CHRONICLE AND HERALD STEAM-PRESS.

MDCCCLXXXII.

Left: Major Poyntz, not satisfied with the standards of the force, issued a number of General Orders. Hair was to be 'a reasonable length', boots were to be worn instead of shoes and decorated truncheons were to be scraped clean and varnished. Soon after he took over as Chief Constable he issued a new booklet setting out guidance for the management of the constabulary, replacing the booklet issued by McHardy in 1849. Poyntz also issued Force Orders, which every officer was obliged to read, listing full details of any disciplinary offence, the name, rank and station of the officers concerned, the punishment awarded and very often his own comments as to the conduct of the officer. This system was stopped with the appointment of the next Chief Constable, Captain Showers. *(Essex Police Museum)*

Below: Pages from the new booklet, outlining the rules of conduct for constables. *(Essex Police Museum)*

about they can hardly fail to know it, and in such case will inform one another, taking such steps, by watching or otherwise, as may seem most likely to lead to detection.

68.—Inspectors and Sergeants are responsible that none of the Constables or any unauthorised person, become acquainted with the night duty arrangements.

69.—Whenever Inspectors or Sergeants have charge of stations or lock-ups, they will be guided by directions and instructions under these heads as detailed for the Superintendents, and all general orders and rules of conduct are applicable to every member of the Force, whatever his rank.

70.—Superintendents, Inspectors, and Sergeants in charge of stations or lock-ups are to be careful that persons charged with murder or other serious offences are not locked up with other prisoners who may be under confinement, but are to be placed under the care of a Constable, who is to be specially instructed that he has no right whatever to interrogate prisoners, or question them with a view to obtaining answers which may be used in evidence against them. It is his duty, nevertheless, not to discourage any statement a prisoner may desire to make; on the contrary, he should make a careful note of it, and if necessary it may be given in evidence.

Constables.

RULES OF CONDUCT.

71.—The Chief Constable recommends young Constables, who at first feel their duties irksome, not to be readily discouraged, but to bear in mind that, if they desire in any way of life to improve their position, they must be ready to work hard, and to bear with some trials, and that the Police service does not present greater difficulties than any other employment.

72.—The principal purposes for which a Police Force is established being the prevention and detection of crime, the suppression of vagrancy, and the maintenance of peace and good order, it will be the imperative duty of every Member of the Constabulary to exert himself to the utmost for the attainment of these ends; remembering always, that as the security of persons and of property is intrusted to his keeping, and the maintenance of public tranquillity confided to his charge, he should at all times set an example, in his own person, of order, integrity, and propriety of conduct.

73.—Every Constable should bear in mind, that on the maintenance of strict discipline the efficiency of the Force will mainly depend; and he is encouraged to hope to rise to the higher degrees by activity, intelligence, and good conduct. To this end he must make it his study to recommend himself to notice, by a diligent discharge of his duties, and strict obedience to the commands of his superiors; good conduct in these respects being considered the first qualification for command.

74.—The Constabulary are to understand that they are to treat every Justice of the Peace with the utmost attention and respect. They are, on all occasions, to be civil and attentive to persons of every rank and condition; and to endeavour, by orderly and regular habits, and a zealous and impartial discharge of their duties, to gain the approbation of the well-conducted of all classes.

75.—All Constables, whether on or off duty, are strictly forbidden to enter into conversation referring to the Service, particularly with strangers; and, when on duty, they are to avoid conversing with any person, except with the view of obtaining information which may assist them in the performance of the duty in which they are at the time engaged. They will also be extremely careful not to interfere, on any occasion, unnecessarily; when required to act, they are to do so firmly and resolutely.

76.—When giving evidence in a Court of Justice, Constables are to stand upright, in the position of attention. They are to give their evidence with perfect impartiality and with a clear and unhesitating voice.

77.—The Constables must remember that no qualification is more essential than a perfect command of temper. They are never to suffer themselves to be moved by any

Edward McLean Showers succeeded Poynt as Chief Constable on 3 July 1888. Born in Moulmein, India, Showers was commissioned into the 95th Derbyshire Regiment. He was a Superintendent in the Devon Constabulary before becoming Chief Constable of Exeter Borough in 1886. Showers was one of the first officers to receive the King's Police Medal. He retired in 1915, but was then appointed Acting Chief Constable of Colchester Borough, while Captain Stockwell (the borough Chief Constable) rejoined his regiment for the duration of the war. Showers died in 1925. *(Essex Police Museum)*

Clacton police station was built in 1892. The population of Clacton in 1891 was only 1,900 and only two constables were stationed in the town. However, it was a thriving seaside resort and during the summer months the numbers increased with holiday makers, so police reinforcements were brought in from Walton, St Osyth and Weeley. When the police station was opened, a Sergeant and two further constables were stationed in the town. *(Essex Police Museum)*

Right: PC 50 Frederick Brown, a former labourer, joined the force on 19 December 1864. During his service he was stationed at Billericay, Rayleigh, Vange and Hockley. Shown here with his daughter, he proudly displays the Merit Badge awarded to him on 1 January 1873 for distinguished conduct in assisting in the apprehension of four notorious poachers. *(Essex Police Museum)*

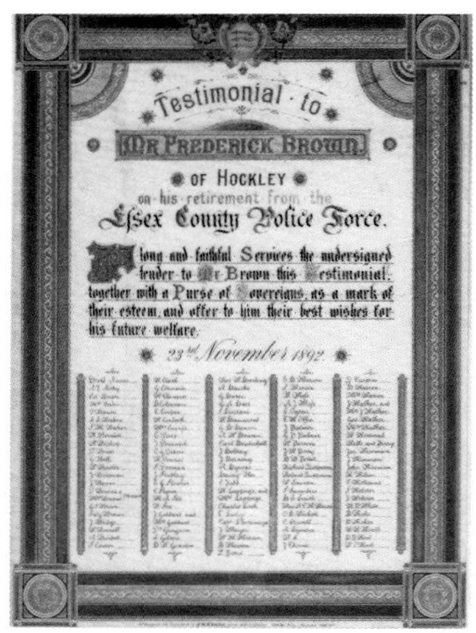

Testimonial · to
Mr Frederick Brown
of Hockley
on his retirement from the
Essex County Police Force.

long and faithful Services the undersigned tender to Mr Brown this Testimonial, together with a Purse of Sovereigns, as a mark of their esteem, and offer to him their best wishes for his future welfare.

23rd November 1892.

Above right: Brown retired on pension on 4 March 1891. He was held in such high esteem by the residents of Hockley that on his retirement they presented him with an illuminated testimonial, together with a purse of sovereigns. It shows the names of those parishioners who contributed towards the presentation. *(Essex Police Museum)*

Acting Sergeant Adam Eves joined the Essex County Constabulary at the age of 20, and in March 1877 was appointed Constable No. 63. He served at various stations throughout the county before being promoted to the rank of Acting Sergeant and posted to Purleigh in January 1891. On the evening of Saturday, 15 April 1893, Constable Eves set out on his usual patrol of the district. The next day his body was found lying at the bottom of a ditch in 6 inches of water. He had suffered dreadful injuries. Four local men, well known in the locality and each with previous convictions for theft and poaching, were arrested and two of them, brothers John and Richards Davis, were found guilty of murder and sentenced to death. Richards was reprieved but John payed the ultimate price. The men had been involved in the theft of corn from a local farm and Eves had surprised them as they were making their way home with the stolen corn. *(Essex Police Museum)*

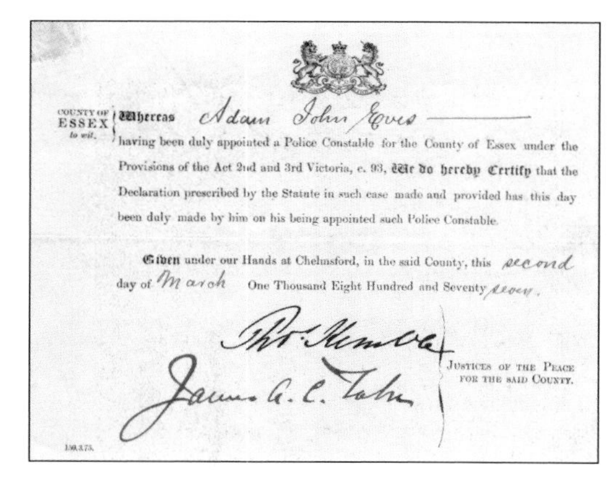

COUNTY OF ESSEX to wit. Whereas Adam John Eves having been duly appointed a Police Constable for the County of Essex under the Provisions of the Act 2nd and 3rd Victoria, c. 93, We do hereby Certify that the Declaration prescribed by the Statute in such case made and provided has this day been duly made by him on his being appointed such Police Constable.

Given under our Hands at Chelmsford, in the said County, this second day of March One Thousand Eight Hundred and Seventy seven.

Thos. Kemble
James A. C. Tolm
Justices of the Peace for the said County.

Above: The certificate appointing Adam Eves as a constable on 2 March 1877. *(Essex Police Museum)*

Right: The grave of Adam Eves in Purleigh churchyard.

Superintendent Samuel Hawtree joined in 1864 after transferring from the Metropolitan Police, where he had served for five years. He was promoted to the rank of Superintendent in November 1880, and was in charge of Southend in 1894. He died in 1918. *(Essex Police Museum)*

WILFUL MURDER

WANTED

For the Murder of Florence Dennis at Southend-on-Sea, 24th June. 1894

JAMES CANHAM READ

Cashier, Royal Albert Docks. London.

Age 39, Height 5ft 7in,
Hair Brown,
Moustache Slight Brown,
Small Side Whiskers,
Eyes Brown and prominent,
Complexion Fresh.
Two Upper Front Teeth project slightly,
One overlaps the other.

DRESS,
Dark Brown Hard Felt Hat,
Short Black Coat and Vest,
Light Grey Trousers,
Walks Quickly,
Is of very smart and Gentlemanly appearance.

Has a Gold Watch engraved inside case "Presented to Mr. James Canham Read by his fellow Clerks, Royal Albert Docks, London."

WARRANT ISSUED.

Information to be sent to
SUPT. HAWTREE, Southend-on-Sea.

FRANCIS & SONS, Printers, &c., 56, High Street, Southend and Rochford.

A wanted poster issued in 1894 for James Canham Read, a married man with eight children who was wanted for the murder of his pregnant mistress, Florence Dennis, at Southend. Read was subsequently arrested, convicted of the offence and hanged at Chelmsford Prison in December 1894. *(Essex Police Museum)*

Superintendent Lindsay Fulcher is pictured seated in the Chief Constable's Belsize motorcar, after it had been delivered to Braintree for its twelve months' divisional trial. The car was sold in 1923 for £100. *(Essex Police Museum)*

Above: 'The Scorchers'. This photograph, taken at Clacton, shows officers proudly displaying their new mode of transport. *(Essex Police Museum)*

Left: This photograph shows Sergeant Joseph Hurrell (1874-1901) and was part of a series taken by Frederick Spalding, a well-known photographer. Hurrell was promoted to the rank of Sergeant in October 1891 and the photograph is believed to have been taken at Danbury, where he was stationed. The girl in the picture is in fact his daughter. *(Spalding Collection – photograph by courtesy of the Essex Record Office)*

Left: Undercover work in 1901. The officers are PC Arthur Collins (right), who served from 1883 to 1915, and PC Frederick Lancum. Although a number of officers were employed on detective duty from 1888, it was not until 1919 that Essex announced the creation of a detective and enquiry department. In 1932 they became the Criminal Investigation Department (CID) under the control of Detective Superintendent George Totterdell. *(Essex Police Museum)*

Below: In 1899 the Standing Joint Committee (responsible for the administration of the force) decided that the existing headquarters at Old Court, Arbour Lane, Chelmsford were not adequate and around £9,000 would be needed to rectify structural defects in the building. A new site was needed and the SJC purchased a three-acre piece of land in Gaol Lane (now Sandford Road), for £1,250. A competition was held with a prize of £100 for plans for the new headquarters. The winner was a Chelmsford man, Mr George E. Clare. *(Essex Police Museum)*

By September 1903 the building was complete and comprised a lodge, Chief Constable's house and stables, a main block, recruits block and further stables. The total cost was £18,000. The new headquarters were known as New Court and are still in use today. At this time the strength of the Essex Constabulary stood at 1,040 men. *(Essex Police Museum)*

Opposite: In 1903 the Essex Constabulary were involved in the search for Miss Camille Cecille Holland at Moat Farm, Clavering, who had disappeared in 1899. Her remains were found and Samuel Herbert Dougal was charged with her murder and subsequently executed at Chelmsford Prison. The officers are pictured with Miss Holland's dog, Jacko. When Jacko died, he was stuffed and eventually given to Essex Police Museum. Detective Sergeant David Scott is seated on the left. The other officers are PCs Fell (seated), Lindsay (with beard) and Field. Scott reached the rank of Superintendent. *(Essex Police Museum)*

Above left: Camille Holland. *(Essex Police Museum)*

Above right: The decayed body of Camille Holland recovered from Moat Farm. A post-mortem revealed she had been shot. The remains were identified by the shoes she was wearing, which are now exhibited in the Essex Police Museum. *(Essex Police Museum)*

To mark the coronation of George V, a number of police officers were awarded the 1911 Coronation Medal. Among the recipients was the Assistant Chief Constable of the Special Constabulary, A.F. Royds. *(Essex Police Museum)*

Harlow police station decorated for the coronation of King George V, on 22 June 1911. *(Essex Police Museum)*

FORM No. 92.

Supt. ~~Insp.~~ ~~PS.55~~ ~~21~~

1952

FORM OF APPLICATION

FOR EMPLOYMENT IN THE ESSEX POLICE.

Date 5th November 1912

Name of Applicant George Henry Rookwood Totterdell

Full Address 2 Lea Road Cresent Road
Brentwood Essex

Date of Birth 2nd July 1892

Place of Birth Eastwood Essex *Occupation* Painter

Height without Shoes or Stockings 5 ft ft. 10½ in. *Married or Single* Single

Chest measurement 33 - 35½ *inches.* *Number of Children* Nil

Previous Police or other Public Service 2nd Battalion Grenadier Guards from 27th August 1912 to 11th October 1912 Purchased discharge

Name and Full Postal Address (in Candidate's own handwriting) of not less than three persons, including present or last Employer, **and of Police of District;** *also, if possible, that of a Minister, Magistrate, or other Public Officer who are willing to bear testimony to the character of the applicant.*

Name.	Full Postal Address.	Period of knowing the Candidate.	
		From the Year.	To the Year.
Mr J. A. Humprey	Belle Vue Gt Leighs Chelmsford	1911	1912
Mr J. G. Fawsey	28 Wakering Avenue Shoeburyness	1906	1912
J Millbank Esqr J.P.	High St Shoeburyness	1907	1912
Rev Ellis Jones	The Rectory Shoeburyness	1908	1912
Sergt. Swann	Brentwood	1911	1912

Candidates must be 5ft. 9in. without shoes and measure 36 inches round chest underneath shirt.

George Totterdell applied to join the Essex Constabulary in 1913. Pictured here is his application form with the names of five people who would vouch to his good character. *(Essex Police Museum)*

FORM No. 56.

ESSEX POLICE.

Southend Division.

Frederick Ferry P.S. 57. reports
P.C. 173. G. Totterdell 3rd Class
for having on the
23rd day of May 1913.
omitted to attend two conference points. viz. a 1. Am. and a 1.30. Am. at Westcliff-Bridge. and absenting himself from his beat from 1. Am. till 1.30. Am. and being in a Porters room at the Westcliff Railway Station during that time

Superintendent [signature] with respect to the above charge, reports that this Constable should have left the Railway Station after seeing the 12.55 am train in, and patrolled Hamlet Court Road, then attend the 1.20 am train, afterwards attend the 1.30 C.P. on the Bridge, but going into the Porters room he was neglecting his beat. The 1 am C.P. has probably been made at the Railway Station sometimes when the Sergt visiting has also attended the train.

[signature] Supt.

states in explanation that I attended my 1am on Railway Station as stated on Night duty list I went in the Porters room & saw the 1-20am train in & then I came to the foot of Westcliff Bridge & made the 130am point as stated also on night duty list. When asked by Sergt Ferry why I omitted the 1am point I replied I was at my 1am he replied you were not It not made on the Station

Geo: Totterdell PC 173

N.B.—As the Chief Constable cannot always personally inquire into a complaint, the Officers charging and charged should make their reports and explanations as complete as possible. The Chief Constable's decision and remarks are to be read to the Officer charged. Any Officer is at liberty to apply to see the Chief Constable personally with reference to any complaint against him, but he must be prepared to pay any expenses incurred if his representation or explanation is frivolous.

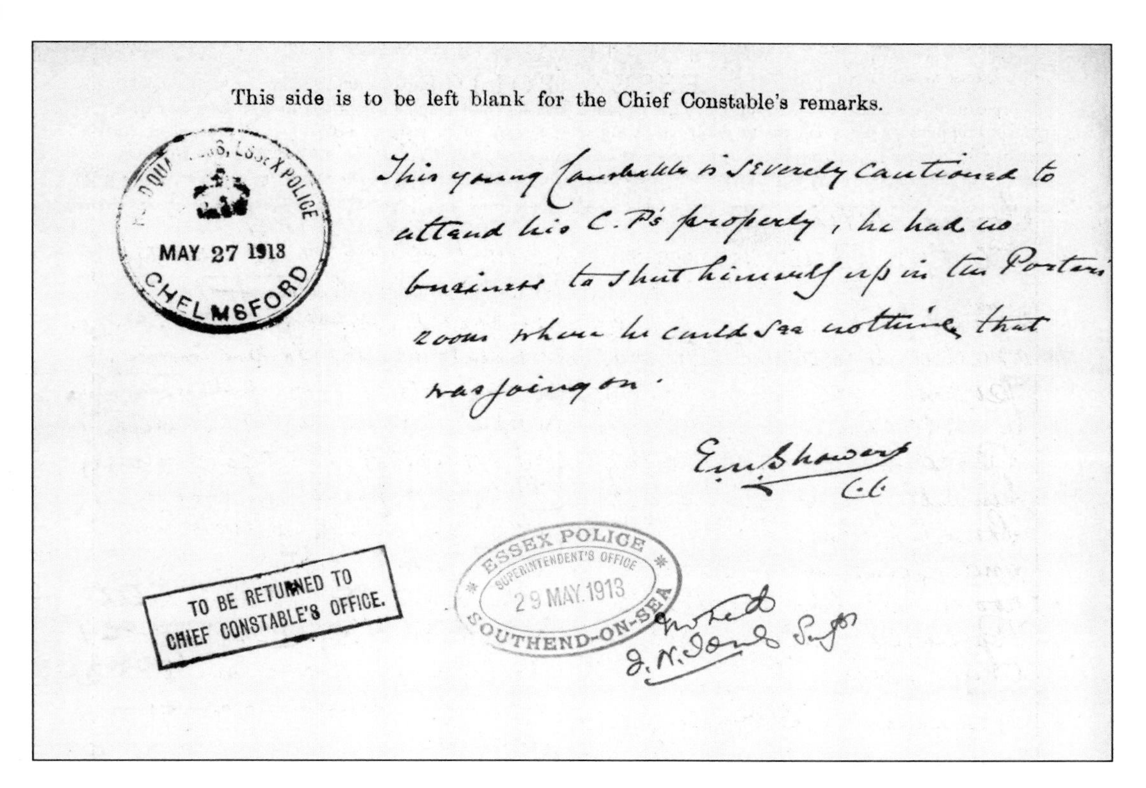
This side is to be left blank for the Chief Constable's remarks.

MAY 27 1913

CHELMSFORD

This young Constable is severely cautioned to attend his C.P's properly, he had no business to shut himself up in the Porters' room where he could see nothing that was going on.

C.C.

ESSEX POLICE

SUPERINTENDENT'S OFFICE

29 MAY 1913

SOUTHEND-ON-SEA

TO BE RETURNED TO CHIEF CONSTABLE'S OFFICE.

Opposite page and above: A duty report submitted by PC Totterdell when he was stationed at Southend, explaining why he missed a conference point. His explanation was not accepted by the Chief Constable, who wrote, 'This young constable is severely cautioned to attend his C.P.'s properly, he had no business to shut himself up in the porters' room, where he could see nothing that was going on.' Totterdell was the first officer in Essex to hold the rank of Detective Superintendent and retired in 1952. He wrote a book about his life called *Country Copper.* His two sons became police officers in Essex, but during the Second World War, whilst serving together in the Royal Navy, their ship was sunk and they both died. *(Essex Police Museum)*

The police station in the Guildhall, Harwich had become unsuitable and a decision was made to build a new one. Harwich police station was completed in 1915 and is still in use to this day. The cost of the building was just under £7,000. *(Essex Police Museum)*

Left: The pony and trap used by the Superintendent at Latchingdon; the motorcar was still a rarity in the police service when this picture was taken in 1916. *(Essex Police Museum)*

Below left: At the outbreak of the First World War, the strength of the force stood at only 450 officers and there was a need to recruit a volunteer police force to aid the regular officers. It was resolved that no fewer than 500 special constables should be available for duty, with a reserve list of others available if required. It is interesting to note that although officially they were the Essex County Constabulary, they often used the term 'Essex Police' instead, a name that would not be officially adopted until 1974. *(Essex Police Museum)*

Below: A warrant card issued to special constables in August 1914. *(Essex Police Museum)*

ESSEX POLICE.

SPECIAL CONSTABLES

As it is very desirable that during the War there should be a **Volunteer Police Force to aid the County Police** throughout the County in the preservation of peace and good order, all those not within the limits of age prescribed for the Territorial Force who are willing to serve **(without remuneration)** are asked to enrol their names at the nearest Police Station with as little delay as possible. They will only be asked to serve in their own towns or parishes. Their principal duties will be keeping good order in Towns and Villages, Guarding Telegraph Wires, Reservoirs and Water Supplies and Bridges, and keeping a sharp look-out for spies belonging to the enemy. Where a wide area is to be covered, **Volunteers should be found who are willing to supply Motor Cars or Motor Cycles** for the purpose of keeping up communication between different parts, and, possibly, of transporting men from one place to another.

The service will be voluntary, but it will be under the control of the Home Office, and its operations will be regulated by the terms of the Police Act. It will be composed of British Citizens of good physique and not within the limits of age prescribed for the Territorial Force, who will form themselves into groups or squads, serving under a Sergeant of their own nomination, who will be responsible for the discipline and duty spells of his squad. The spell of duty will be four hours per day, and arrangements will be made to avoid interference as far as possible with the men's ordinary occupations. The Special Constables will be employed in the neighbourhood of their homes, and will make their own arrangements for food. They will be equipped with a truncheon and will wear an armlet on the left arm when on duty. It is desirable that they should act under the immediate control of the Chief Constable and in close connection with the Police, and, when they are sworn in, directions to this effect should be given them by the Justices by whom they are appointed.

Superintendents and Inspectors in charge of Police Stations will make arrangements for having the Volunteer Police sworn in before a Justices as soon as possible after registration, and a list is to be kept at each Station showing the names of the Special Constables for each Town and Village throughout the County of Essex, and Superintendents of Divisions will furnish the Chief Constable with a copy of same as early as possible. Truncheons and armlets to be served out proportionately to each place according to the number that would be on duty at one time.

No.	Name	Address	Occupation

E. M. SHOWERS, Capt.,
Chief Constable of Essex.

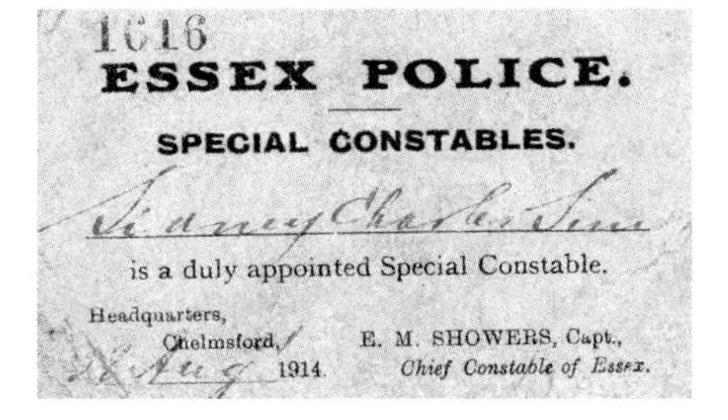

ESSEX POLICE.

HEADQUARTERS,
CHELMSFORD, April, 1915.

TO ALL RANKS OF THE ESSEX POLICE.

G.O. 815.—Under every circumstance a farewell is a sad incident, and when it severs for ever associations which have lasted for nearly 27 years between Officers and Men of this Force and myself, as Chief Constable, it becomes a very painful ordeal.

You have been with me in trouble and in peace, and the Essex Police have always won the highest esteem and praise from all classes, and were never known to shirk their duty, and this I feel sure they will continue to do as long as any of them remain in the Force.

Since this terrible War commenced in August, you have all had little or no leave, and have had to work very long hours in the performance of many arduous duties in this important Eastern County, all of which you have carried out most ably and to my entire satisfaction.

I thank both Officers and Men most sincerely and gratefully for their loyalty and devotion to the County and myself personally. Any successes I may have achieved during my Service in Essex are entirely due to the assistance I have received from them.

I would especially like to mention the valuable Services of my Deputy-Chief Constable, Mr. Raglan Somerset, and my Superintendent and Chief Clerk, Mr. George Hastings, who have ever been untiring in their devotion to me and their work, and I owe them both a deep debt of gratitude. I grieve to think I shall not be here to welcome back those of my men who have gone to the Front to fight for their KING and COUNTRY, some of whom, alas! I know will never return to us.

I have no hesitation in saying that I feel sure you will all render to the new Chief Constable, Captain J. A. Unett, D.S.O., the same faithful service you have given me.

It is with real sorrow and reluctance I say "Good-bye" to a Force which is second to none in the Kingdom, and I hope you will sometimes remember me, for, wherever you are, you will be in my thoughts till the end of time.

Yours faithfully,
E. M. SHOWERS, Capt.,
Chief Constable of Essex,
1888-1915.

In 1915 Captain Showers, who had been Chief Constable for nearly twenty-seven years, had to retire on account of his age (sixty-nine). In General Order No. 815 he expressed his thanks to the members of the force and wished them well for the future. However this was not to be the end of his career as he was appointed the Chief Constable of Colchester Borough for the duration of the war while the Chief Constable, Captain Stockwell, returned to the colours. *(Essex Police Museum)*

Left: Officers of the Brightlingsea section photographed in 1915. Sergeant Josiah Scott (seated), with PCs Garrett, Chaplin and Havers. During the First World War, police officers were not exempt from conscription and from a total of 450 men, no fewer than 154 left for the war. An additional strain was put on those who remained by the fact that recruiting to the police force was halted for the duration. Special constables were appointed to fill the gaps left by those police officers on war service. They were placed under the supervision of Captain Matthew Finch, a retired army officer and a Justice of the Peace. *(Essex Police Museum)*

Below: Members of the special constabulary from Great Wakering. They were not issued with uniforms, but were given armbands (worn on the left arm), to signify their authority, and a truncheon. *(Essex Police Museum)*

Special constables stationed at Romford and photographed in 1916. They continued to work at their day jobs but were expected to perform four hours duty a day in the vicinity of their homes. They were eventually issued with a peaked cap, police cape and a whistle, and had their own rank structure, with a Chief Special Constable in charge. Notice the two boy scouts sitting in the front row; they were used as messengers. *(Essex Police Museum)*

Duty List

OF

Special Constables.

Halstead, 1914.

Left and below: The booklet issued giving details of the beats that the constables were expected to patrol and the times they were expected to be present at a conference point. *(Essex Police Museum)*

Duty List of Special Constables,

HALSTEAD

Constables will patrol the respective Beats and be at the Points mentioned at the times stated in the following tables.

A Beat Patrol between Queen's Hall, Star Stile, Cangle Farm, to Worlds End Corner.
B „ „ „ „ Bentalls Barn, Stoney Lands, Potash Farm.
C „ „ „ „ Deans Hall, Pebmarsh Corner, Stoney Lands.
D „ „ „ „ Snowden Fen, Stanstead Hall, Langley Mill.
E „ „ „ „ Balls Chase, Letches Farm, Plaistow Green.
F „ „ „ „ Mount Hill, Bourne Brook, Plaistow Green.
G „ „ „ „ Chappel Hill, White Ash Green, Cut Hedge.
H „ „ „ „ Wash Farm, Brook Street Farm, White Ash Green.
I „ „ „ „ Gas Works, Does Corner, Pearmans Hill.
J „ „ „ „ Dead Lane, Parsonage Street, Firwood.
K „ „ „ „ The Cedars, Police Station.
L „ „ „ „ Factory Terrace, Kings Road, Mount Pleasant, Trinity Street.
M „ „ „ „ Clover's Mill, Box Mill, Frost's Mill, North Street.
N „ „ „ „ Colchester Road, Snowden Fen, Knights Farm.
O „ „ „ „ High Street, Balls Chase, Blue Bridge, Snowden Fen, Dead Lane.

Dr John Salter was a doctor and a magistrate before he was appointed Chief Special Constable at Witham. Salter kept a diary for eighty-two years, his entries recorded important events such as the Boer War, the First World War and the sinking of the *Titanic*. Salter's diary entry for 25 August 1914, at the age of seventy-four, records: 'Aug. 25. Sworn in as a special constable.' He was awarded the Special Constabulary Long Service Medal in 1919, for his service during the First World War. *(Essex Police Museum)*

Dr Salter's special constabulary armband, denoting his rank as Chief Special Constable. Badges of rank for the special constabulary were issued from 1915. *(Essex Police Museum)*

Above: These two photographs were taken at Epping in 1916 at the scene of a fire. The constable in the right-hand picture is wearing an armband on his left arm, which appears to display a crown on it. It is not clear what this signifies, as there are no other photographs of the period showing officers wearing it. *(Essex Police Museum)*

Below: A guide book issued by the National Union of Women Workers. *(Essex Police Museum)*

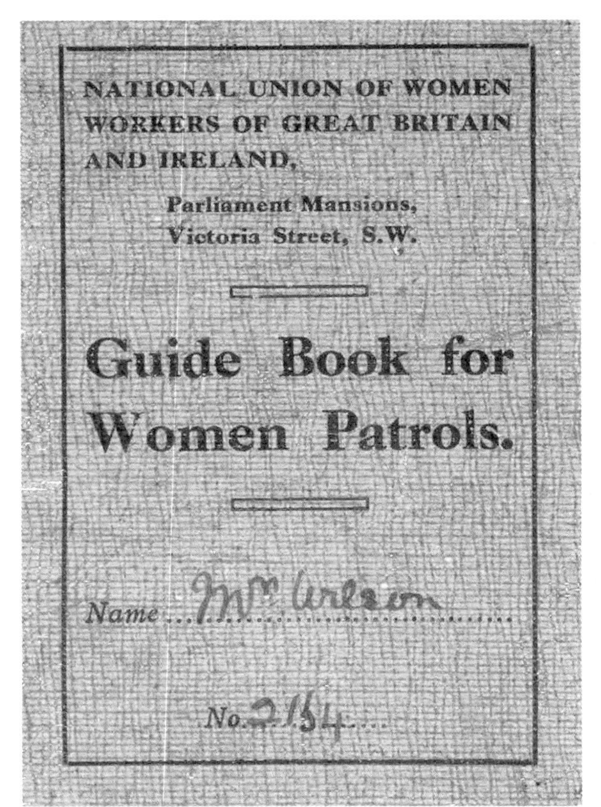

NATIONAL UNION OF WOMEN WORKERS OF GREAT BRITAIN AND IRELAND,

Parliament Mansions,
Victoria Street, S.W.

Guide Book for Women Patrols.

Name ...Mrs Wilson...

No. 2154

Above and opposite: The First World War gave women their first real chance to become involved in police work. Alice Wilson (above) joined the National Union of Women Workers in 1918. She was stationed at Romford police station with one other woman, Dora Jordan (pictured opposite). They were the first women to work as 'officers' for the Essex Constabulary. Their main role was to deal with women and children, and Alice and Dora spent a lot of their time walking the beat and liaising with welfare organisations. They both left Romford in 1919 as they were no longer required. Despite pressure from various organisations including the Women's Institute, it was not until 1946 that women were employed as police constables in Essex, with full powers. *(Essex Police Museum)*

DIAGRAMS OF

BRITISH & GERMAN AIRSHIPS

ALL DRAWN TO SCALE

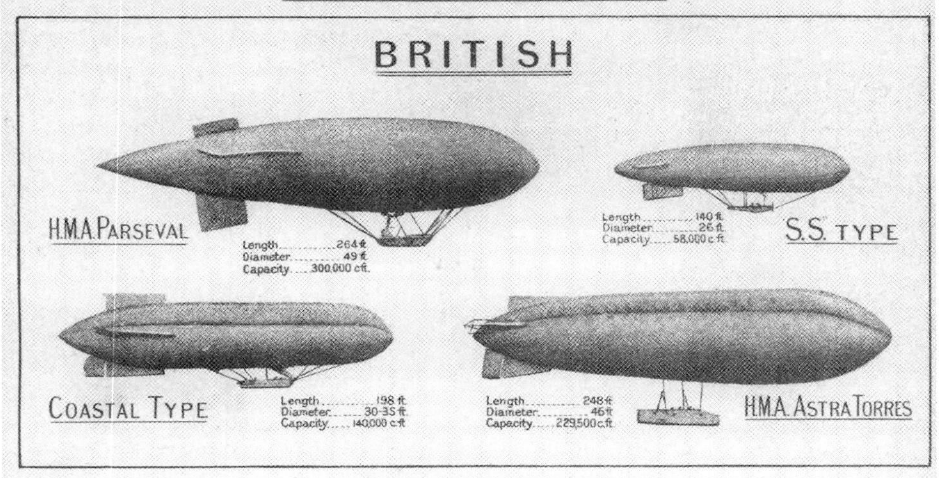

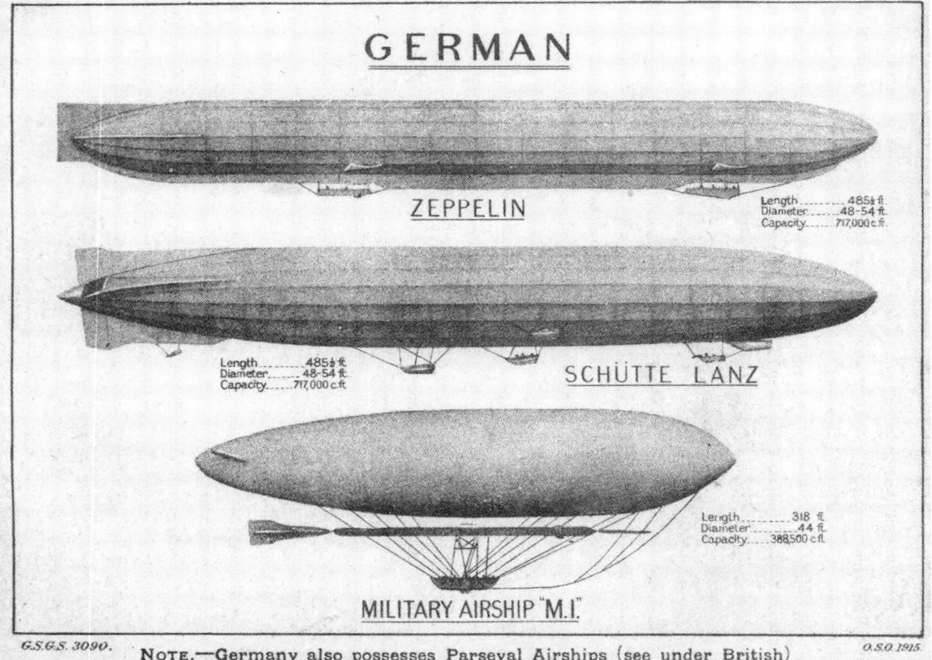

G.S.G.S. 3090. O.S.O. 1915.

NOTE.—Germany also possesses Parseval Airships (see under British) but neither they nor the M. type are likely to be often seen in Great Britain.

Opposite: During the First Worl War, numerous raids were made on London and the Home Counties (including Essex) by German airships, and many civilians were killed and property damaged. Police officers were issued with this chart to try and distinguish between British and German airships. In September 1916, two Zeppelins were brought down over Essex, one at Great Burstead, near Billericay and another at Little Wigborough, near Colchester. Souvenirs from the crashed craft were sought after, and despite attempts by the military to safeguard them, parts of the aluminium structure were taken. *(Essex Police Museum)*

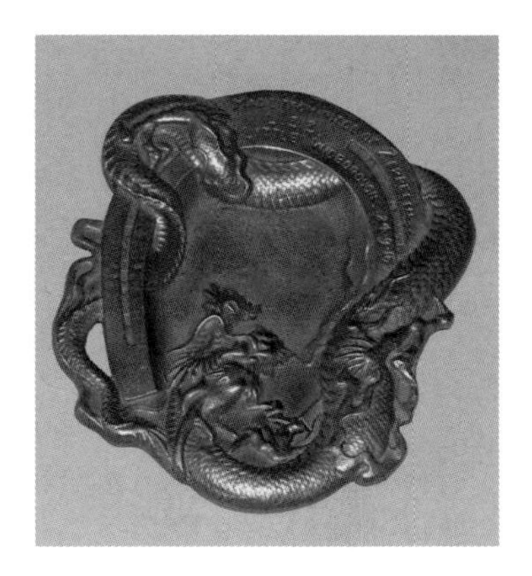

Above left: Part of the Little Wigborough Zeppelin, skilfully crafted into an ashtray. It bears the inscription, 'Made from piece of Zeppelin L33, Little Wigborough 24.9.16'. *(Essex Police Museum)*

Above right: The names of all the special constables who served during the First World War were recorded for each Petty Sessional Division throughout the county and were displayed in the courts. The board above records the names of those who served within the Witham Petty Sessional area. It has been estimated that some 10,000 special constables were appointed in Essex between 1914 and 1919. One special constable, Corporal Revd Joseph Thomas, lost his life when he drowned whilst on duty in December 1914. *(Essex Police Museum)*

Badges issued to special constables in the First World War. The one on the left was issued to constables, the middle was for supervisors and on the right is a senior officer's cap badge. *(Essex Police Museum)*

John Alfred Unett was appointed Chief Constable of Essex on 8 May 1915. Born in 1868, he served in the 3rd Hussars from 1889 and was promoted to Captain in 1898. He began his police career with the City of London Police, and was Superintendent and Chief Clerk in Hertfordshire between 1909 and 1912. He was appointed Chief Constable of Preston borough in 1912, serving there until he came to Essex. Soon after his appointment he restructured the special constabulary and introduced procedures to deal with speeding motorists, which involved police officers with stop watches, checking the time taken for motorists to travel along a quarter mile stretch of road. He died in post on 6 December 1932. *(Essex Police Museum)*

THE

TRUNCHEON

Vol. I. DECEMBER, 1928. No. 7.

The Periodical of the Essex Constabulary.

J. Dutton, Printer and Stationer, Chelmsford.

The Truncheon magazine, described as 'The Journal of the Essex County Constabulary', was started in November 1925 and was to continue until 1948 (with a break during the Second World War). It was eventually replace by the *Essex Police Magazine*, which commenced in November 1952. This magazine was to continue until summer 1989. *(Essex Police Museum)*

The General Strike of 1926 was a busy time for the police service as a whole. There were a number of strikes in Essex and extra police had to be drafted into the docks in Grays Division to prevent trouble. This photograph shows seven officers who were awarded the Merit Badge for their work during this period. *(Essex Police Museum)*

Officers in Clacton Division photographed in 1926. *(Essex Police Museum)*

Left: Sergeant Ernest James Brooks, who joined the constabulary in 1895. For many years he was responsible for training recruits. He retired in 1923 and in 1926 he was appointed an Inspector in the Special Constabulary for instructional purposes. *(Essex Police Museum)*

Below: A helmet plate displaying the officer's collar number. *(Essex Police Museum)*

A group of new recruits at headquarters in 1926, with Sergeant Brooks seated in centre of the front row. Training of recruits took place at Police Headquarters, before the officers were sent out to their stations. *(Essex Police Museum)*

PC George Gutteridge pictured with his daughter Muriel. In the early hours of 27 September 1927, two men, Frederick Guy Browne and William Henry Kennedy, were driving a stolen car at Stapleford Abbotts, when PC Gutteridge signalled them to stop. While Gutteridge was questioning them Browne fired two shots at him from the driver's seat. The constable staggered backwards and fell in the road. Browne got out of the car, telling Kennedy, 'I'll finish the bugger' and, standing over PC Gutteridge, fired a shot into each of his eyes. Browne and Kennedy drove off to London, leaving PC Gutteridge dead in the road. It was a crime that appalled the nation and made headline news. Browne was arrested in January 1928, still in possession of the murder weapon. Kennedy was arrested in Liverpool five days later for car theft, after trying to shoot the arresting officer. Kennedy admitted being with Browne in the stolen car but insisted that Browne had done the shooting and that he could do nothing to intervene as he was scared of Browne. Browne's defence was that he was at home on the night of the murder and this was borne out by his wife and landlady. However, the Old Bailey jury convicted them both of being jointly responsible for the murder. Browne was hanged at Pentonville and Kennedy at Wandsworth. *(Essex Police Museum)*

PC Gutteridge's grave at Brentwood. *(Essex Police Museum)*

A helmet plate painted black and worn at night. *(Essex Police Museum)*

William Howlett joined in 1886 and rose through the ranks and was appointed Deputy Chief Constable in 1922. He retired in 1926 after forty years police service, but died shortly after retiring. *(Essex Police Museum)]*

John Crockford, who was appointed the first permanent Assistant Chief Constable of Essex in 1935. A former farm labourer, he joined the force in 1911 and was one of the earliest members of the Detective and Inquiry Department (CID). He retired in 1953. His younger brother, George, was Chief Constable of Southend Borough from 1935 to 1939. *(Essex Police Museum)*

Francis Jonathan Peel was appointed Chief Constable on 1 May 1933. Born in 1897, he saw war service with the Royal Field Artillery, where he won the Military Cross. A graduate of Cambridge University, he joined the Liverpool City Police in 1920. In 1931 he joined Bath City as an Assistant Chief Constable and eventually became Chief Constable. Knighted in 1959, he retired in December 1962, and died on 6 December 1979. *(Essex Police Museum)*

Captain Peel (seated fourth from the right) and the senior officers of the force. To his left sits John Nightingale, who had been appointed Assistant Chief Constable in 1953 and who would eventually become Chief Constable. *(Essex Police Museum)*

In rural areas police officers lived in the community they served and their house was often used as the local police station. Here is Copford police station photographed in 1931. *(Essex Police Museum)*

The cast-iron plaque placed on police buildings. *(Essex Police Museum)*

A group of officers stationed at Witham, *c.* 1938. *(Essex Police Museum)*

The 1920s and '30s saw an increase in the number of motorcars on our roads, and it was left to the police to deal with the accidents which inevitably occurred. Here a constable investigates such a collision with the help of an AA patrolman in 1934. *(Essex Police Museum)*

This photograph was taken at Chelmsford bus station and the caption on the rear just says 'Bus Strike 1937'. *(Essex Police Museum)*

The Home Office initiated the idea of motor patrols to deal with the increasing use of motor vehicles by criminals. In 1931 ten 549cc Triumph motorcycles were purchased, each costing £45, together with a number of cars. When Captain Peel became Chief Constable in 1933 he reviewed the use of motorcycles, preferring cars, and by December the motorcycle section had been disbanded. *(Essex Police Museum)*

A photograph showing members of the traffic department with two Ford V8 patrol cars, 1938. *(Essex Police Museum)*

Officers from the motorcycle section: PC Arthur Cole (above) and PC Cyril Pinch (left). Crash helmets were not worn, the riders being given flat caps to wear.

Romford police station, built in 1892. Romford was policed by the Essex Constabulary from 1840 until 1965. With the creation of the Greater London Council, the Romford Division became part of the Metropolitan Police on 1 April 1965. One hundred and thirty-nine officers were transferred to the new force. The station was rebuilt in 1965 and is still in use. *(Essex Police Museum)*

A driving school was based at Witham police station in the late 1930s. Shown here are PCs Oakley, Leonard, Goose and Smith. PC Goose is displaying his Merit Star, which he was awarded in 1934 for endeavouring to arrest three men for burglary. *(Essex Police Museum)*

A group of recruits who joined on 1 August 1939, just before the outbreak of the Second Worl War, photographed at HQ. Seated is Assistant Chief Constable Crockford. On his left is Inspector Wombwell, the recruits' instructor. By December 1939, 101 officers had been recalled to the colours. In 1941 a further seventy-three officers volunteered and with conscription in 1942, another 117 officers were called up. In total 291 officers served in the armed forces, twenty-four of whom were killed in action. *(Essex Police Museum)*

No. 11

ESSEX COUNTY COUNCIL.

AIR RAID PRECAUTIONS.

This is to Certify that

Police Sergt. C Perry

has qualified as an INCIDENT OFFICER

and Instructor

A. L. Seaman

Sub-Controller.

Date 3/4/44

In 1936 the Home Office began a programme of training courses on air-raid precautions and Essex sent Inspector George Hodges to be trained as an instructor; he then trained other members of the constabulary. Pictured is a certificate issued to Sergeant C. Perry, showing he was a qualified Incident Officer and Instructor for Air Raid Precautions. *(Essex Police Museum)*

BRANCHES: LONDON, BIRMINGHAM, MANCHESTER, LEEDS, GLASGOW.
AGENTS IN PRINCIPAL COUNTRIES THROUGHOUT THE WORLD.

HOFFMANN
Registered Trade Mark

BALL-AND-ROLLER-BEARINGS
STEEL-BALLS-AND-ROLLERS

TELEPHONE: 3151 (FIVE LINES)
TELEGRAMS: HOFFMANN, CHELMSFORD
CODES USED: A.B.C. 5TH EDITION BENTLEY PHRASE, BENTLEY 2ND PHRASE, MARCONI AND WESTERN UNION 5 LETTER.

THE HOFFMANN MANUFACTURING CO. LTD.

CONTRACTORS TO THE ADMIRALTY, WAR OFFICE AND INDIA OFFICE

G. HODGES ESQ.,
INSPECTOR.
ESSEX COUNTY CONSTABULARY,
HEAD QUARTERS,
CHELMSFORD.

CHELMSFORD.

26th July, 1938.

YOUR REF.
IN YOUR REPLY PLEASE QUOTE
OUR REF. GB/AES.

Dear Sir,

I am sorry that owing to ill health I was unable to attend the last two lectures of the course on Air Raid Precaution.

I would however, state how very much I appreciated the manner in which you conducted these lectures and the very helpful information given.

I am returning the service Respirator No.173 loaned me during the lectures.

Again thanking you, I remain,

Yours faithfully,
THE HOFFMANN MANUFACTURING COMPANY LIMITED.

Bass.

CHIEF POWER ENGINEER.

A letter from Hoffman Manufacturing Co. Ltd of Chelmsford, thanking Inspector Hodges for his lectures to the firm. Hoffmans were a major manufacturer of ball and roller bearings, vital to the war effort. The factory suffered many air raids with workers killed. *(Essex Police Museum)*

In November 1940 a German air raid took place over Chelmsford. Just after 7 p.m. the Police Headquarters was hit and two officers, PC Alexander Scott and PC Maurice Lee, who were on guard duty, were killed. The photographs clearly show the damage caused by the bombs. *(Essex Police Museum)*

Above left: Inspector Butcher outside a heavily sandbagged Ongar police station during the Second World War. The effects of the war brought enormous pressures to bear on the police. To assist the regular officers, special constables, auxiliaries consisting of a First Reserve of retired officers, and a War Reserve (those men who would otherwise have been called up for military service) were recruited. *(Essex Police Museum)*

Above right: A poster issued by Captain Peel for the attention of aliens. *(Essex Police Museum)*

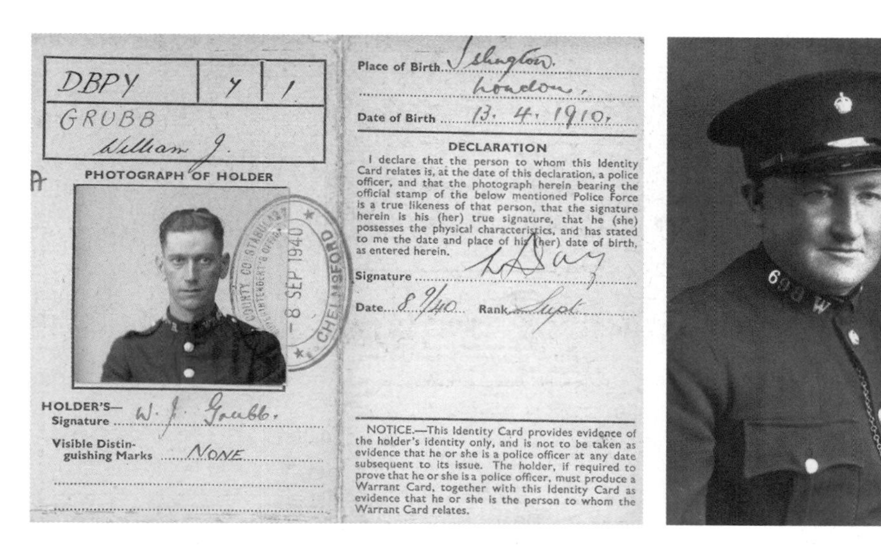

DBPY | Y | 1

GRUBB

William J.

PHOTOGRAPH OF HOLDER

HOLDER'S— Signature W. J. Grubb.

Visible Distinguishing Marks NONE

Place of Birth Islington, London.

Date of Birth 13. 4. 1910.

DECLARATION

I declare that the person to whom this Identity Card relates is, at the date of this declaration, a police officer, and that the photograph herein bearing the official stamp of the below mentioned Police Force is a true likeness of that person, that the signature herein is his (her) true signature, that he (she) possesses the physical characteristics, and has stated to me the date and place of his (her) date of birth, as entered herein.

Signature

Date 8/9/40 Rank Supt.

NOTICE.—This Identity Card provides evidence of the holder's identity only, and is not to be taken as evidence that he or she is a police officer at any date subsequent to its issue. The holder, if required to prove that he or she is a police officer, must produce a Warrant Card, together with this Identity Card as evidence that he or she is the person to whom the Warrant Card relates.

Above left: An identity card issued in 1940 to War Reserve constable William Grubb, who served between 1940 and 1945 at Chelmsford and Galleywood. *(Essex Police Museum)*

Above right: A War Reserve constable, believed to be Sidney Thompson who served at Tilbury between 1944 and 1945.

Above left: Special constables also played an important part during the war. Pictured here are a group of special constables from Wickford, photographed in 1942.

Above right: After the war many officers who had served in the colours returned to the force. Pictured above is PC Stanley wearing the ribbon of the Distinguished Flying Cross (DFC) awarded to him whilst serving in the Royal Air Force Volunteer Reserve (RAFVR). He retired in the rank of Inspector in 1956. *(Essex Police Museum)*

A inspection taking place of special constables. *(Essex Police Museum)*

Above left: A picture of a Sergeant and three War Reserve constables, believed to have been taken at Chelmsford. War Reserve constables were committed to full-time employment and were paid the same pay as regular officers – £4 10*s* per week. They wore the same uniform with the addition of the words 'War Reserve' on the sleeve. They also wore flat caps instead of helmets. *(Essex Police Museum)*

Above right: A Christmas party held by the Essex Constabulary in 1942 for local police families. *(Essex Police Museum)*

During the Second World War, women were employed as Women Auxiliary Police Constables. They worked as clerks and telephonists at Headquarters and at some stations. They were given training in basic police duties, first aid, self-defence and air-raid precautions. However, they were not sworn in as police officers and therefore could not carry out arrests. Shown, from left to right, are Doris Turner, Betty Harcourt and Molly Rand. It was not until 1946 that Essex employed its first women police officers. *(Essex Police Museum)*

By the KING'S Order the name of

William Stratford,

Special Sergeant, Essex County Constabulary,

was published in the London Gazette on

9 January, 1945,

as commended for brave conduct in
Civil Defence.

I am charged to record His Majesty's
high appreciation of the service rendered.

Prime Minister and First Lord
of the Treasury

Special Sergeant William Stratford was commended for brave conduct in January 1945, for the part he played in successfully rescuing three people from a demolished house in Maldon on 20 September 1944. Pictured is the citation, which appeared in the *London Gazette. (Essex Police Museum)*

Home Office,
Whitehall,
S.W.1.

8th January, 1945.

Sir,

I am directed by the Secretary of State to inform you that the Chief Constable of Essex drew his attention to your gallant conduct on 20th September, 1944, when you succeeded in rescuing three people from a demolished house in Acacia Drive, Maldon, although you were suffering from shock.

Mr. Herbert Morrison felt that your courage and devotion to duty were deserving of high praise and he took steps to bring the matter to the notice of His Majesty The King, who was graciously pleased to give orders for the publication of your name as having received an expression of Commendation for your services.

The notice will appear in a list to be published as a Supplement to the London Gazette on the evening of 9th January, 1945.

I am, Sir,
Your obedient Servant,

A. Maxwell.

Special Sergeant W. Stratford.

The letter informing Sergeant Stratford of his award. *(Essex Police Museum)*

Joan Hurley served as an auxiliary policewoman between 1941 and 1946. She was stationed at Epping and often had to cycle to work in complete darkness because of the blackout regulations that were in force. In 1946 she joined as a regular police officer serving until 1970, having attained the rank of Sergeant. *(Essex Police Museum)*

George Percy Sutton joined Essex in 1919. During the Second World War he was a military forces liaison officer. He became divisional commander of Romford Division, then the biggest division in the county. He was the first holder of the newly introduced rank of Chief Superintendent. The photograph shows him in the uniform of an Assistant Chief Constable, to which he was promoted in 1953. He retired from the force in 1959, having served for forty years. *(Essex Police Museum)*

The official programme issued for the victory celebration, which took place on 8 June 1946. *(Essex Police Museum)*

Right and below: In March 1947 Harlow New Town was designated as one of a ring of eight new planned communities around London. People from London were in desperate need of housing as the city had suffered extensive bombing in the war. In 1949 the Master Plan received formal assent and by August of that year the first tenants had moved to Harlow. In 1957 a decision was made to build a new police station in the town centre to replace the station at Old Harlow, which had been in use since 1908. *(Essex Police Museum)*

The full potential of using dogs was only realised in the 1930s and it was not until September 1953 that Essex purchased two dogs from Surrey Constabulary. The first two dog handlers in Essex were Dan Hare (who eventually became dogmaster in the Royal Hong Kong Police), and Peter Cousins. In 1970 a purpose-built dog section was erected at Sandon and is still in use today. Here we see PC Peter Cousins with his doberman pincer Remoh.

Above: A group of dog handlers. Sergeant Dan Hare is in the front row (seated).

Right: Road Safety was an important part of the work of the police in Essex, and various initiatives were introduced to reduce the number of accidents on the road. This pamphlet gave details of serious accidents on the county's roads. *(Essex Police Museum)*

A double-decker bus was pressed into service as a travelling Essex Road Safety Exhibition. *(Essex Police Museum)*

PC Jim Woolnough dealing with a road traffic accident in 1959. The dangers posed by motor vehicles were ever-present and a number of police officers were killed whilst dealing with these types of incident on the roads of Essex. *(Essex Police Museum)*

PC Sidney Dodd served in the Royal Artillery throughout the Second World War. On joining the force in September 1949, he was posted to the Grays Division, and as a married man with a young son, he became a detached beat officer at Horndon-on-the-Hill. One Sunday evening in February 1957, PC Dodd was cycling along the Stanford-le-Hope bypass when he was knocked down and killed by a drunk driver. *(Essex Police Museum)*

In 1914, the Port of London Authority suggested that Kent, Essex and the Metropolitan Police should link up to police the lower reaches of the Thames from Dagenham to the sea, which at that time were unsupervised. However, Essex resolved that in the absence of statutory authority the matter should be allowed to rest, and it was not until 1948 that the Chief Constable, Captain Peel, decided to consider the use of a launch on the River Thames. Pictured are (left) police launch *Watchful*, photographed in 1959 and (right) police launch *Alert*, based at Tilbury. *(Essex Police Museum)*

Above: The 42ft purpose-built police launch *Vigilant II*, which came into service in 1959 to replace the original launch *Vigilant*, which had commenced duties in 1949. *(Essex Police Museum)*

Left: Police divers were part of the unit and would be called in to carry out underwater searches. *(Essex Police Museum)*

John Cyprian Nightingale was born in 1913 and, after graduating from University College, London with a BA in Classics, he joined the Metropolitan Police as a constable in 1935. He was selected for accelerated promotion under Lord Trenchard's scheme at Hendon, becoming a Junior Station Inspector. He served in the Royal Navy in the Second World War. In 1950 he joined the directing staff of the police training centre at Ryton-on-Dunsmore, near Coventry, and was appointed Commandant of Eynsham Hall Police Training Centre in 1953. He returned to the Metropolitan Police in 1956, but in 1958 he was appointed Assistant Chief Constable of Essex. He became Chief Constable in 1962 and remained in charge until his retirement in 1971. He was knighted in 1975 and died in 2007. He was the last person to reside in the Chief Constable's house at Headquarters. *(Essex Police Museum)*

Nightingale when he was a Junior Station Inspector in the Metropolitan Police, 1937. In 1941 he was awarded the British Empire Medal for bravery for rescuing a man from a collapsed building. (Note the badges of rank which are no longer used.) *(Essex Police Museum)*

A photograph of John Nightingale as a Superintendent, shaking hands with Viscount Montgomery of Alamein in the 1950s. *(Essex Police Museum)*

The assize court was held in Chelmsford twice a year, when the judges came to try the most serious cases. Here, in October 1965, the judges are escorted from Chelmsford Cathedral back to the Judges' Lodgings. Assize courts and quarter sessions were replaced in 1971 by the now-familiar crown courts. *(Essex Police Museum)*

Many villages had their own policeman. Here is PC Tony Cooper outside the police house at Margaretting, setting out to patrol his beat, *c.* 1965. *(Essex Police Museum)*

Two wireless cars were taken into use in 1936. However, the messages were transmitted by morse code from Scotland Yard and the system only worked in the divisions where the signals could be received. In 1946 the Home Office agreed that Essex could go ahead with its own transmitters, and masts were erected at Headquarters, Great Bromley, Warley and Saffron Walden. A communications department was formed in Essex in 1948 with an information room (seen here) being located at Police Headquarters at Chelmsford. Ten Wolseley cars became the first Essex vehicles to be fitted with two-way radios. Experiments with personal issue two-way pocket radios began in 1965 in the Chelmsford Division. *(Essex Police Museum)*

Left: Frank Joslin working in the information room during the 1960s. *(Essex Police Museum)*

Below: In 1966, the Home Office carried out experiments with military helicopters to see whether helicopters had a place in police work. Police observers were trained and Essex was one of the forces chosen to take part in the experiment, being allowed the use of a helicopter for two weeks in March 1967. The trained observers were all Chief Inspectors or Inspectors. Shown here are John Postan, Donald Harmer, George Manning and Harry Rand. It was not until 1990, however, that Essex acquired its very own helicopter. *(Essex Police Museum)*

From left to right: Olive Butler, Dorothy Hodges, Peggy Sandford and Iris Kemp in 1966. Peggy Sandford transferred to Surrey Constabulary in 1967 as a Chief Inspector. *(Essex Police Museum)*

TWO

COLCHESTER BOROUGH CONSTABULARY

1836–1947

Left: Following the 1835 Municipal Corporations Act the Colchester Borough Police was formed in 1836. The force initially consisted of a Superintendent and nineteen men. The Superintendent received 21*s* per week and the constables, aged between twenty-five and forty, 7*s* per week, and each was supplied with a great coat, truncheon and rattle. The rattle was to be used only in case of fire, the escape of a felon, or when a constable was in danger of being overpowered. By 1837 the force was reduced to only eight men, although the salary of each was 16*s* per week. Colchester Borough was to remain in existence for 111 years before being compulsorily amalgamated with Essex in 1947. *(Essex Police Museum)*

Below: A page from the Incident Book for 1842, showing clothing and equipment given to each officer. Handcuffs and rattles appear not to have been issued! *(Essex Police Museum)*

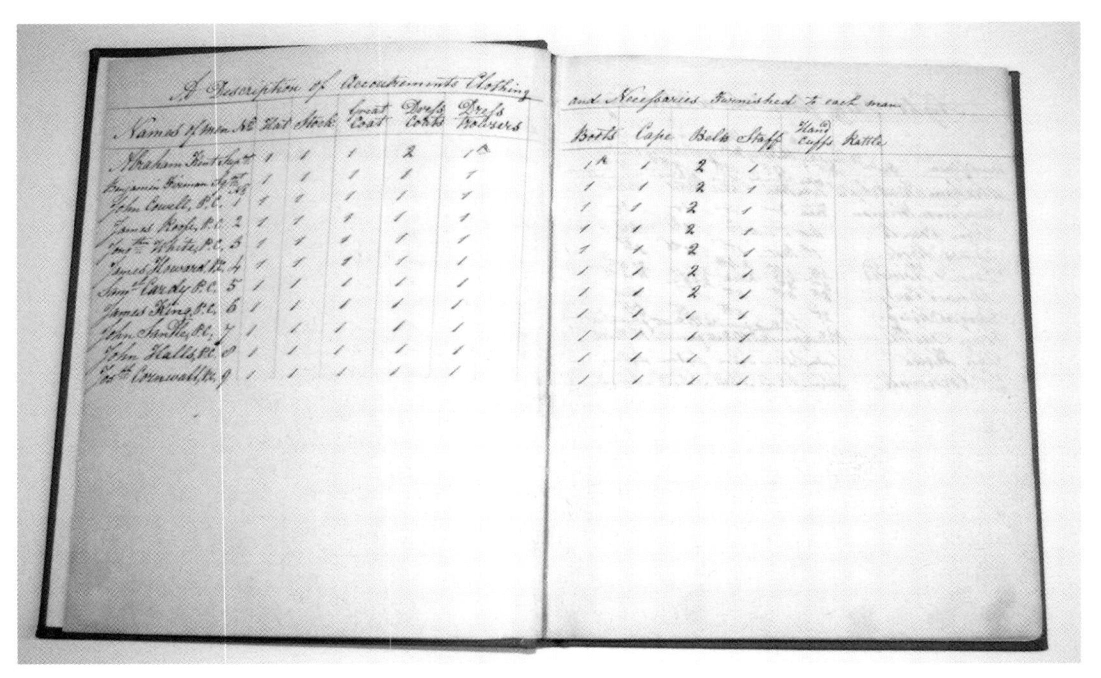

A Description of Accoutrements Clothing and Necessaries Furnished to each man

Names of men	No.	Hat	Stock	Great Coat	Dress Coats	Dress Trousers	Boots	Cape	Belts	Staff	Hand Cuffs	Rattle
Abraham Hunt Supt		1	1	1	2	1	1	1	2	1		
Benjamin Freeman Sgt		1	1	1	1	1	1	1	2	1		
John Cowell, P.C.	1	1	1	1	1	1	1	1	2	1		
James Roofe, P.C.	2	1	1	1	1	1	1	1	2	1		
Jonth White, P.C.	3	1	1	1	1	1	1	1	2	1		
James Howard P.C.	4	1	1	1	1	1	1	1	2	1		
Saml Cardy P.C.	5	1	1	1	1	1	1	1	2	1		
James King, P.C.	6	1	1	1	1	1	1	1	1	1		
John Santle, P.C.	7	1	1	1	1	1	1	1	1	1		
John Halls, P.C.	8	1	1	1	1	1	1	1	1	1		
Josh Cornwall, P.C.	9	1	1	1	1	1	1	1	1	1		

Sunday March 20th 1842

Rank No &c	Names of men	No of Beats	Remarks
Sup't	Abm Kent	Patrol	Visited the men on their Beats &c
	Benjn Firman	on Duty at the Office and general Duty of the town	
No 1	Jno Cowell	2nd	
2	Js Roofe	3rd	
3	Jonthn White	Of Duty	
4	Js Howard	1st	
5	Saml Cardy	4th	
6	Js King	5th	
7	Jno Sandle	Patroles	Old Heath and to new Quay &c
8	Jno Halls	Patroles	Lexden Bottle end &c
9	Jth Cornwall	Patroled	Mile end and Brays wick &c from 6 in the evening until 2 in the Morning

all the Public Houses and Bear Houses Visited During the Morning service and Reported to be Orderly and all Right
The Houses at Lexden and Bottle end Visited by Halls
The Houses at Mile end Visited by Cornwall
the Houses at, greenstead Harwich Road &c Visited by Sandle
Reported to all Orderly &c A Kent

Monday March 21st 1842

Rank No &c	Names of men		Remarks
Sup't	Abraham Kent	on Duty at the Office Patroled, Visited the men	
	Benjamin Firman	general Duty of the town &c	
No 1	John Cowell	2nd	
2	James Roofe	3rd	
3	Jonathan White	1st	
4	James Howard	Of Duty	
5	Samuel Cardy	4th	
6	James King	5th	
7	John Sandle	Patroles	Old Heath greenstead &c
8	John Halls	Patroles	Lexden Bottle end &c
9	Jth Cornwall	Patroled	Mile end Brays wick &c from 6 in the evening until 2 in the morning

Abm Kent

Details of the officers and the beats that they patrolled and any incidents they dealt with. It would appear at this time there were only eleven serving officers: Abraham Kent, who was the Superintendent, and ten constables. *(Essex Police Museum)*

The mounted section, led by Sergeant Wynn, is pictured here being inspected by the Chief Constable, Mr S.R. Midgley, in front of Colchester Castle, *c.* 1910. Colchester did not own horses but loaned them from the local cavalry for ceremonial duties. *(Essex Police Museum)*

Above: A photograph of the force, *c.* 1900. The two officers on the extreme right of the photograph are constables from the River Colne section of the force. *(Essex Police Museum)*

Left: Captain Hugh Charles Stockwell was Chief Constable of Colchester Borough from 1912 until 1915, when he asked to rejoin his old regiment for the duration of the First World War. During his absence Captain Showers, who had retired as Chief Constable of Essex in 1915, was asked to take charge of the force. As a Lieutenant-Colonel, Stockwell returned to take command in March 1919. At this time the force consisted of a Chief Constable, one Chief Inspector, five Inspectors, seven Sergeants and forty-three constables. Stockwell served as Chief Constable until the force was forced to amalgamate with Essex on 1 April 1947. *(Essex Police Museum)*

Above: The force paraded ready for inspection. The officers are wearing straw helmets, which were issued for use during the summer months. *(Essex Police Museum)*

Right: This photograph is believed to be of PC 59 Harmon William Hagon, who served in Colchester Borough between 1907 and 1912. He is wearing a duty armband on his left arm. Upon joining he was paid 23*s* 11*d* per week. He was required to provide himself with 'at least one respectable suit of plain clothes which must always be worn when he is off duty'. *(Essex Police Museum)*

Below: A straw helmet. *(Essex Police Museum)*

Above left: Detail of the belt buckle worn by officers. (*Essex Police Museum*)

Above right: A civic ceremony taking place in High Street, Colchester. Mounted officers are providing a fanfare. (*Essex Police Museum*)

The oyster industry was important to Essex and by 1844 the Colne Fishery Co. employed no less than 500 smacks and 2,000 men whilst as many worked in the Blackwater for the Tollesbury and Mersea Co. Some 144 million oysters a year were being sold in the streets of London alone. Seen here is Sergeant Ted Greengrass with PCs Ted Ward and Elijah Ward, and PC Mummery on the cutter *Prince of Wales*, *c.* 1930. *(Essex Police Museum)*

Above and below: In 1891 the Colne River Police were formed as part of the Colchester Borough Police to protect the lucrative oyster fisheries on the River Colne. The force consisted of a Sergeant, Thomas Poole, and three constables, C.G. Simmons, C.F. Absalom and E.J. French, the cost being shared between the oyster industry (three-quarters) and the borough rates (one-quarter). Poole was promoted to Inspector in 1898 and remained in charge of the force until his retirement. The force had a number of boats at their disposal including the *Alert* and *Brisk*, which were built locally at Rowhedge, and a steam launch, *Viking*, which was replaced in 1902 by another, much grander steam launch, *Edward VIII*. Other boats included the *Raven*, built in 1892, *Victoria*, commissioned in 1897, and *Prince of Wales*. *(Essex Police Museum)*

Police forces were inspected to ensure they were efficient, and to qualify for the grant from the Home Office. Here the mounted section is being inspected by the Chairman of the Watch Committee, and the Chief Constable, *c.* 1905. *(Essex Police Museum)*

Colchester Borough, *c.* 1924. *(Essex Police Museum)*

The water polo team in 1937. *(Essex Police Museum)*

Right: Inspector Drane, born in 1881, joined Colchester in June 1906. He was promoted to Sergeant in 1918 and during the General Strike of 1926 he was put in charge of a group of constables and had to escort a convoy of lorries from Colchester to Whitechapel in London. According to Drane, 'we were right in the thick of it all and were met by lurid threats on every side'. *(Essex Police Museum)*

Far right: The badge worn on Inspector Drane's cap. *(Essex Police Museum)*

Colonel Stockwell was keen to recruit sportsmen into the force, especially boxers. This practice, coupled with the recruitment of a particularly knowledgeable trainer, Syd Humphreys, jelled to produce what, during the 1930s, was regarded as the best police boxing team in Europe. One of the star performers was PC 60 Arthur (Jock) Porter, who won the European Police Heavyweight Championship twice. He is pictured with his trainer, Syd Humpreys, and watched by three colleagues. Jock joined the force in 1937 and served until 1942. *(Essex Police Museum)*

Jock winning the European Police Championship in 1938. *(Essex Police Museum)*

The force boxing team in 1937. *(Essex Police Museum)*

The force rifle shooting team in 1930. Colonel Stockwell is standing in the centre of the back row. As can be seen from the medals worn, the majority had seen military service. *(Essex Police Museum)*

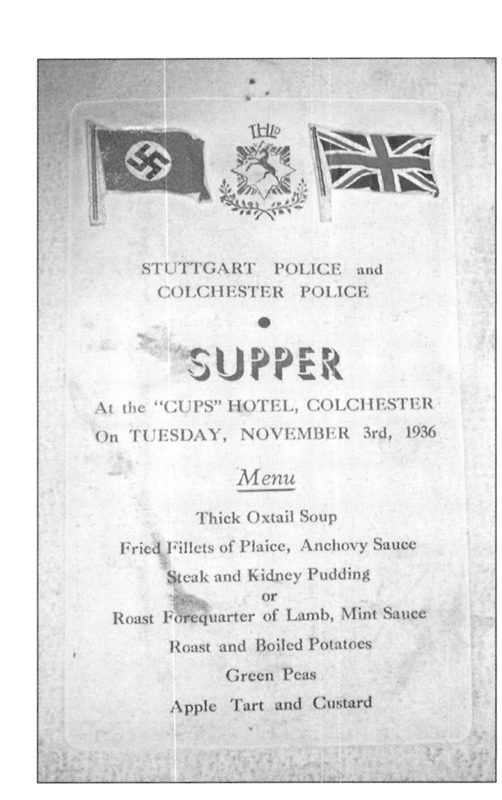

STUTTGART POLICE and
COLCHESTER POLICE

SUPPER

At the "CUPS" HOTEL, COLCHESTER
On TUESDAY, NOVEMBER 3rd, 1936

Menu

Thick Oxtail Soup
Fried Fillets of Plaice, Anchovy Sauce
Steak and Kidney Pudding
or
Roast Forequarter of Lamb, Mint Sauce
Roast and Boiled Potatoes
Green Peas
Apple Tart and Custard

Left: In 1936, Colchester Borough Police entertained a boxing delegation from the Stuttgart Police. This is the menu card for the supper held at the Cups Hotel, showing the German Swastika flag.

Below: A photograph of the two teams taken in the Town Hall, with trainers and officials. *(Essex Police Museum)*

Standing are WPCs D. Sirensen and K. Breen. Seated, from left to right, are WPC V. Sutherland, WPS D. Kirk and WPC I. Clear. Dorothy Kirk had served during the First World War in the Women's Police Service and had spent six years in Hove Borough Police before moving to Colchester. It was the rule at that time that policewomen who married had to leave the force, and so she secretly married David Miller Kirk, a constable in Colchester Borough, in August 1937. He was called up and unfortunately killed on Friday, 16 June 1944, whilst serving as Major with 301 Battery, 127 Field Regiment, Royal Artillery. He was aged thirty-six. Only then did Dorothy admit to the marriage. She applied for a widow's pension, which, because she had broken the rules, caused great consternation and the matter was referred to the Home Secretary. She was granted full pension rights and continued to serve in the force until she retired. David Kirk was the only officer from Colchester Borough to be killed during the Second World War. *(Essex Police Museum)*

BOROUGH OF COLCHESTER

Souvenir

of the HANDING-OVER PARADE

of the

BOROUGH POLICE FORCE

from the

WATCH COMMITTEE

to the

ESSEX STANDING JOINT COMMITTEE

UNDER THE PROVISIONS OF THE

POLICE ACT, 1946

31st March, 1947

WITH THE COMPLIMENTS OF
ALDERMAN E. ALEC BLAXILL,
Chairman of the Watch Committee.

Left: In 1947 the authorised strength of the force stood at seventy-seven, although its actual strength was sixty-one, consisting of a Chief Constable (Colonel Stockwell), one Chief Inspector, four Inspectors, seven Sergeants, and forty-four constables. In addition there was one woman police Sergeant and four women constables. On 1 April 1947 they ceased to be a separate force and were amalgamated with Essex. Pictured is a souvenir brochure from the Handing-Over Parade. *(Essex Police Museum)*

Below: The Colchester team winning the Borough First Aid Cup in the 1950s. Sitting on the right is Chief Inspector Harry Salmon, who served in Colchester Borough between 1919 and 1947, and Essex until 1955. He died in 1996 aged 100. *(Essex Police Museum)*

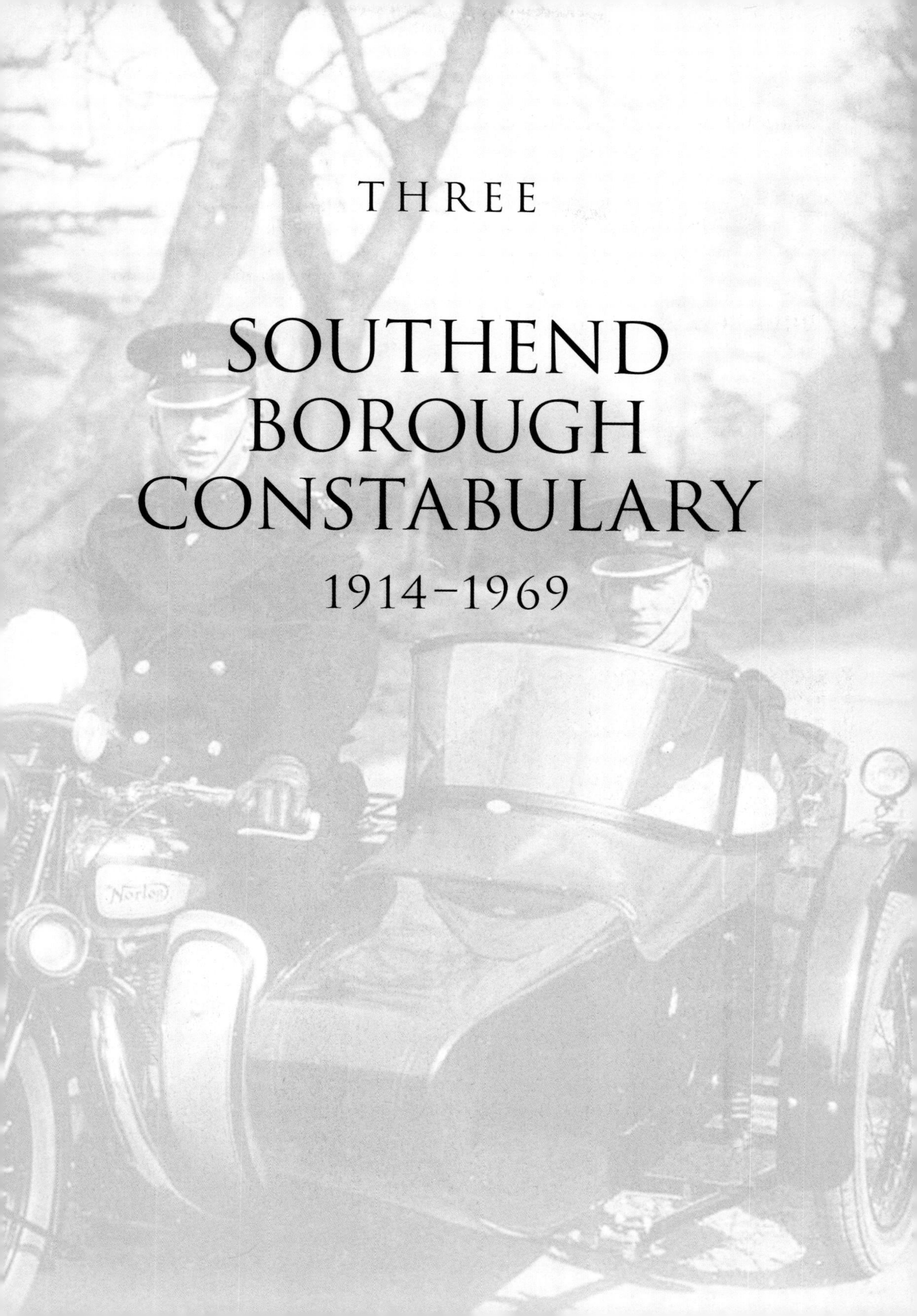

THREE

SOUTHEND BOROUGH CONSTABULARY

1914–1969

This picture, taken outside the old Alexandra Street police station, shows Superintendent Jones and officers of the Essex Constabulary stationed at Southend just prior to the amalgamation. Seated on the right of Superintendent Jones is Detective Inspector Ellis, who later became chief Inspector. In 1914 Southend had been granted county borough status and established its own police force. Henry Maurice Kerslake was appointed Chief Constable. Initially 101 officers were appointed to form the new force, seventy-three of whom came from the Essex Constabulary. Kerslake served from 1914 until his retirement in 1935. *(Essex Police Museum)*

On 1 April 1914, the new force paraded in the yard at the rear of the police station in Alexandra Street, where they were inspected by the Watch Committee. There was at that time no national pay scale for policemen, each force being allowed to fix their own rate of pay. Southend fixed the rate for constables at 26*s* per week on appointment, rising to 34*s* after twelve years' service. This was higher than that paid to their colleagues in Essex. By July 1914 officers were granted one day's leave each week. This helmet plate, issued in 1914, was in fact a white metal star surmounted by a Tudor Crown with a second crown in the centre. Above the central crown on a circular boss was the word 'POLICE' and below a sprig of oak leaves. No records appear to exist to explain why such a helmet plate was adopted, but a suggestion that a delay in getting a die ready due to the First World War does not seem improbable. *(Essex Police Museum)*

The first pattern helmet plate was only worn for twenty-two months and in February 1916 it was replaced by a white metal star with the force title and the arms of the borough in the centre. Another feature that was to appear on this and all subsequent plates was the addition of a wreath imposed over the star. Between 1916 and 1954 black versions of the helmet plates were worn for night duty. These were painted by officers at their own expense and were not manufactured as such. *(Essex Police Museum)*

Mr Kerslake considered first aid to be of the utmost importance and every policeman was required to train in this subject, those qualified wearing a badge on the left sleeve of their tunics. The force was also responsible for providing an ambulance service in the borough, a constable on each tour of duty being detailed as an ambulance officer. He would stand outside Alexandra Street police station and if an ambulance call was received he would go to the fire station, where the fireman responsible for driving the ambulance would be ready. *(Essex Police Museum)*

WE DESIRE on behalf of His Majesty's Government to thank you in common with all others who came forward so readily during the crisis and gave their services to the Country in the capacity of Special Constables.

Stanley Baldwin
PRIME MINISTER.

W Joynson Hicks
HOME SECRETARY.

Downing Street,
May, 1926.

To Mr George M. Drage
COUNTY BOROUGH OF SOUTHEND-ON-SEA
SPECIAL CONSTABULARY.

Left: The force had only been formed a few months when war broke out in August 1914. In total fifty-two men served in the armed forces, of which eight were killed in action. One hundred and twenty special constables were sworn in on 14 August 1914, their numbers increasing during the course of the war. They were equipped in a similar manner to those in Essex. Pictured is a certificate issued by the Government thanking members of the special constabulary for their services. *(Essex Police Museum)*

Below: A group of special constables who served at Southend during the First World War.

Left: Captain Leopold McLaglan was a world champion in Jiu-Jitsu and was invited by the Chief Constable, Mr Kerslake, to train police officers in Southend in the art. Kerslake was impressed and said, 'Apart from the possibility of a loaded firearm, I know nothing that would give a policeman greater confidence and feeling of security in the presence of dangerous criminals, than a knowledge of jiu-jitsu as imparted by you.' Pictured is the handbook written by McLaglan on Police Jiu-Jitsu.

Below: A certificate awarded to PC Frank Chivers in May 1922, who attended a course in the noble art. *(Essex Police Museum)*

DIEU ET MON DROIT

CERTIFICATE OF MERIT

This is to Certify

that Constable Frank Albert Victor Chivers
has attended a Course of Jiu Jitsu Instruction,
held under my personal supervision, at
Southend-on-Sea on 8th ~ 13th May 1922.
and has made himself proficient.

Captain
Leopold McLaglen

Inventor of the New System of Bayonet Fighting as used in the great European War.

ADVANCE AUSTRALIA

ADVANCE NEW ZEALAND

Sergeant Fred Bonnett and members of the Watch Committee looking over a 10hp Hillman Minx Aero motorcar. Southend formed a Road Patrol in March 1931, patrols being undertaken by motorcycle and motorcycle combinations. In 1934 one of the combinations was replaced by a motorcar and was used by the Detective Branch. *(Essex Police Museum)*

PCs Bob Reenan and Bill Thorogood on patrol in a Norton sidecar outfit in 1931. *(Essex Police Museum)*

PCs Eric Tomlinson and Donald Hudson. *(Essex Police Museum)*

A motor patrol enjoying a break outside the Robin Hood Tea Gardens. *(Essex Police Museum)*

The force vehicles at the rear of Alexandra Street police station. *(Essex Police Museum)*

Artists.

Miss Eileen Farrow. (Mezzo Soprano) — Mrs. D. L. Davies. (Accompanist)

Master H. Flewitt. — Special Constable F. Whisstock.

P.s. T. Edwards. — P.c. D. L. Davies.

P.c. A. F. Theobald. — P.c. S. Everett.

The Police Glee Singers.
(Leader: P.c. D. L. Davies. Accompanist: Det. Sgt. W. E. Taylor.)

Toastmaster—Constable S. G. Glasscock.

Southend-on-Sea Constabulary
Recreation Club.

Club Supper

AT

The Middleton Hotel,

ON

Thursday, 3rd December,

1936.

at 6.45 p.m.

Above and below: Southend had a Recreation Club for staff. Here we have the menu card for their Club Supper, held in 1936. Entertainment was provided by various people including 'The Police Glee Singers'. *(Essex Police Museum)*

Menu.

Cream of Tomato.

Fried Fillet of Plaice and Lemon.

Roast Beef or
Boiled Leg of Mutton and Caper Sauce.

Brussel Sprouts. Turnips. Potatoes.

Fruit Salad and Ice Cream.

Cheese and Biscuits.

Toast List.

The King.
Proposed by The President.
(G. R. Crockford, Esq.)

The President.
Proposed by The Chairman of the Club Committe
(P.c. S. G. Glasscock.)
Response by The President.

The Club.
Proposed by H. M. Kerslake, Esq.
Response by The Honorary Secretary.
(Inspector C. K. Sim.)

The Special Constabulary, Ex-Members of the Force, The Visitors and Artists.
Proposed by The Deputy Chief Constable
(A. J. Hunt, Esq.)
Response by W. J. Drake, Esq.
(Special Constabulary)
Ex-Inspector L. Baker.
(Ex-Members of the Force)
His Worship the Mayor,
(ALD. W. MILES, J.P.)
(The Visitors)
Det. Sgt. W. E. Taylor.

The Police Glee Singers, photographed in the 1950s. *(Essex Police Museum)*

PC 99 Victor Theobald and his brother PC 46 Alfred Theobald, photographed in 1938. Alfred was a member of The Police Glee Singers. *(Essex Police Museum)*

During the First World War, Southend had become a target for enemy bombing raids and a number of people were killed in the town. In 1939 Alexandra Street police station was heavily sand-bagged to protect it from bombs. *(Essex Police Museum)*

Members of the CID photographed in 1931. *(Essex Police Museum)*

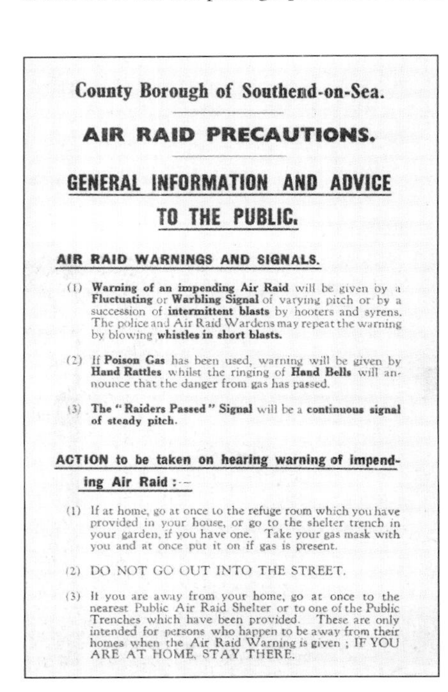

County Borough of Southend-on-Sea.

AIR RAID PRECAUTIONS.

GENERAL INFORMATION AND ADVICE TO THE PUBLIC.

AIR RAID WARNINGS AND SIGNALS.

(1) **Warning of an impending Air Raid** will be given by a **Fluctuating** or **Warbling Signal** of varying pitch or by a succession of **intermittent blasts** by hooters and syrens. The police and Air Raid Wardens may repeat the warning by blowing **whistles in short blasts.**

(2) If **Poison Gas** has been used, warning will be given by **Hand Rattles** whilst the ringing of **Hand Bells** will announce that the danger from gas has passed.

(3) **The "Raiders Passed" Signal** will be a **continuous signal of steady pitch.**

ACTION to be taken on hearing warning of impending Air Raid :–

(1) If at home, go at once to the refuge room which you have provided in your house, or go to the shelter trench in your garden, if you have one. Take your gas mask with you and at once put it on if gas is present.

(2) DO NOT GO OUT INTO THE STREET.

(3) If you are away from your home, go at once to the nearest Public Air Raid Shelter or to one of the Public Trenches which have been provided. These are only intended for persons who happen to be away from their homes when the Air Raid Warning is given ; IF YOU ARE AT HOME, STAY THERE.

Above left: Leaflet issued during the Second World War at Southend, giving general information and advice on what to do if there was an air raid on the town. *(Essex Police Museum)*

Above right: DCI Harry Hempson (seated), who joined the force in 1920. He was promoted to Chief Inspector in 1948 and in 1956 he was awarded the British Empire Medal. He retired in 1964 after forty-four years service. Standing is Detective Inspector Tom Martin. *(Essex Police Museum)*

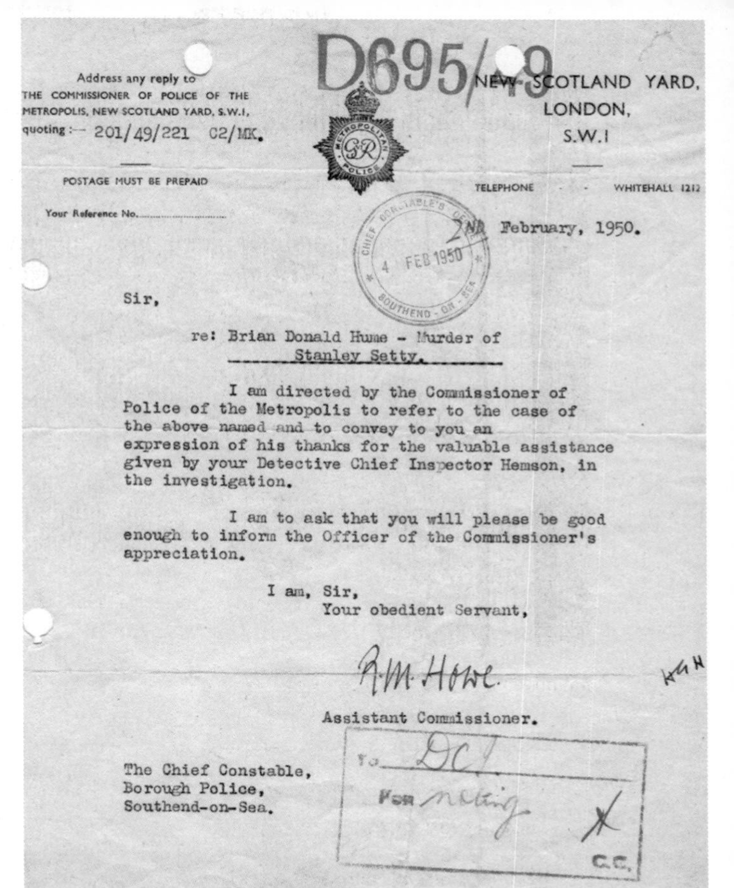

D695/49

Address any reply to
THE COMMISSIONER OF POLICE OF THE
METROPOLIS, NEW SCOTLAND YARD, S.W.1,
quoting :— 201/49/221 C2/MK.

POSTAGE MUST BE PREPAID

Your Reference No.........................

NEW SCOTLAND YARD,
LONDON,
S.W.1

TELEPHONE - - WHITEHALL 1212

CHIEF CONSTABLE'S OFFICE
4 FEB 1950
SOUTHEND-ON-SEA

2nd February, 1950.

Sir,

re: Brian Donald Hume - Murder of
Stanley Setty.

I am directed by the Commissioner of Police of the Metropolis to refer to the case of the above named and to convey to you an expression of his thanks for the valuable assistance given by your Detective Chief Inspector Hemson, in the investigation.

I am to ask that you will please be good enough to inform the Officer of the Commissioner's appreciation.

I am, Sir,
Your obedient Servant,

R.M. Howe.

Assistant Commissioner.

The Chief Constable,
Borough Police,
Southend-on-Sea.

To DCI
For noting
C.C.

A letter of commendation from the Metropolitan Police to DCI Hempson, for his assistance in the investigation of the murder of Donald Setty in 1950. *(Essex Police Museum)*

A photograph taken in April 1938, showing Sergeant Hempson and other officers gaining entry to a burnt-out shop in Nelson Drive, Leigh, the owner of which was found inside having been attacked. *(Essex Police Museum)*

Above left: Sergeant Harry Drage. *(Essex Police Museum)*

Above right: Sergeant George Rushforth. *(Essex Police Museum)*

A group of Southend officers photographed in the 1950s. *(Essex Police Museum)*

Above: The force pictured with their new Chief Constable, Mr William McConnach, in 1953. Mr McConnach, a native of Aberdeen, had joined the Plymouth City Police in 1931 as a constable and rose through the ranks in that force until his appointment to Southend. He was awarded the MBE and retired in 1965. *(Essex Police Museum)*

Right: The Old Comrades Association was formed by Captain John Unett, Chief Constable of Essex, for the maintenance of comradeship and good fellowship between retired officers and those still serving who have more than fifteen years' service. Pictured is the programme for the Silver Jubilee of the Association, held in 1955 at Garon's Banqueting Hall, Southend. The Old Comrades Association continues today. *(Essex Police Museum)*

Above: Sergeant Sam Perry (left) was awarded the British Empire Medal, and PC John Beckett (right) was awarded the Queen's Commendation for Bravery, for disarming a man carrying a loaded shotgun. The distinctive white helmets were introduced into the force in 1962 for wearing during the summer months when the officers could be seen clearly amongst the crowds of holidaymakers. *(Essex Police Museum)*

Left: PC Ruickbie on 'Gresham' in 1967. *(Essex Police Museum)*

Southend Police Mobile Column. These columns were formed in the 1960s in various police regions in order that, should a nuclear war occur, they could be withdrawn to a safe location ready to go in and police the devastated area. The column, under the command of a Superintendent, consisted of 100 men and women. *(Essex Police Museum)*

The force vehicle fleet drawn up for inspection in the early 1960s. This photograph was taken at Shoebury Garrison. *(Essex Police Museum)*

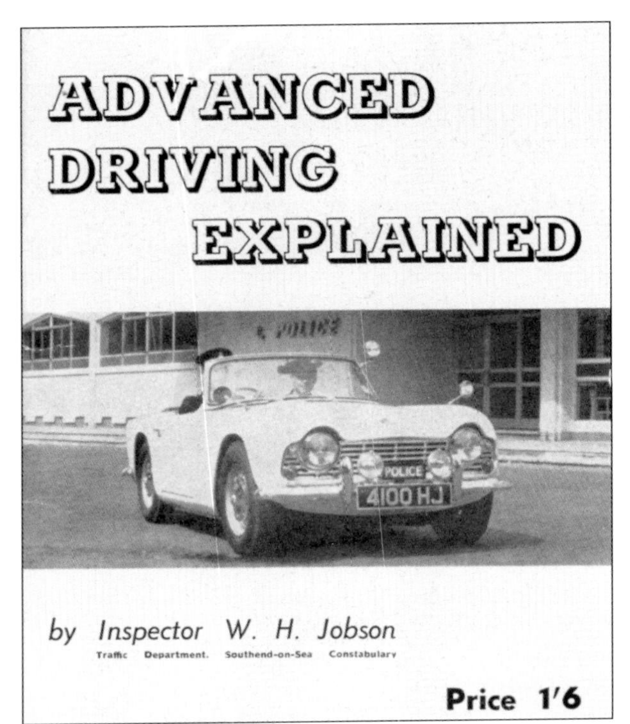

Left: Driver training was an important aspect of a police officer's instruction. The booklet 'Advanced Driving Explained' was written by Inspector William Jobson, who was a serving Southend officer. *(Essex Police Museum)*

Below: In 1956 a sea rescue patrol was instituted; the crew consisted of a driver and two constables, all qualified lifesavers. The vehicle patrolled the sea front for two hours each side of high tide and was equipped with life-saving lines, harness and floats. *(Essex Police Museum)*

The sea rescue patrol with the rubber dingy in 1959. *(Essex Police Museum)*

PC Mick Grover and Tom Whalley from the sea rescue patrol launching the dingy. *(Essex Police Museum)*

A Traffic Department Triumph TR4 being driven by PC Les Bennett in 1966. The passenger is PC Eric Kidwell. *(Essex Police Museum)*

The vehicle fleet and officers being inspected by the Mayor of Southend at the official opening of the police station in 1962. *(Essex Police Museum)*

A constable using one of the police pillars on the sea front at Pier Hill. Southend also had a number of 'tardis' type police boxes. They were used before the advent of personal radios and had been introduced in 1924. *(Essex Police Museum)*

Superintendent Bill Burles. *(Essex Police Museum)*

Above: The motorcycle patrol section on the occasion of the visit by Her Majesty the Queen Mother to Southend on 31 October 1967. *(Essex Police Museum)*

Left: In 1933, John Mitchell, a local solicitor, gave a cup and medal to be awarded annually for 'the most conspicuous act of personal courage performed in the course of his duty by a member of the police force, fire brigade, or any servant of the Corporation'. It has been awarded to a number of police officers. The medal is still awarded annually if there is a suitable recipient. Pictured here is Sergeant John Robinson, who joined in 1948, proudly displaying his medals, including the Mitchell Medal, which he received for a sea rescue in 1956. The medal was worn on the right-hand side of the uniform. (*Essex Police Museum)*

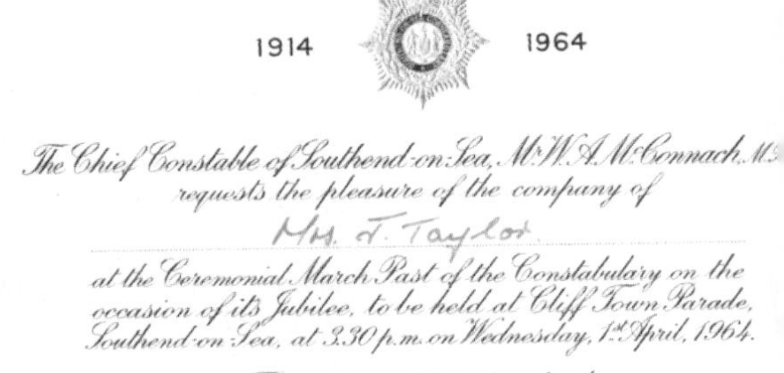

1914 1964

The Chief Constable of Southend-on-Sea, Mr W. A. McConnach, M.

requests the pleasure of the company of

Mrs. J. Taylor

at the Ceremonial March Past of the Constabulary on the occasion of its Jubilee, to be held at Cliff Town Parade, Southend-on-Sea, at 3.30 p.m. on Wednesday, 1st April, 1964.

The salute will be taken by the

Lord Lieutenant of the County of Essex, Sir John Ruggles-Br

Bt., C.B., O.B.E.

R.S.V.P. not later than
25th March 1964.

P.

Above left: An inspection by the Mayor of Southend. *(Essex Police Museum)*

Above right: An invitation to the ceremonial march past of the force to celebrate their Golden Jubilee on 1 April 1964. The salute was taken by the Lord Lieutenant of Essex, Sir John Ruggles-Brise. *(Essex Police Museum)*

Sir John inspecting the force accompanied by the Chief Constable, Mr McConnach, and Superintendent James Devlin. *(Essex Police Museum)*

Wearing their distinct white helmets, members of the Southend Borough Constabulary proudly parade through the streets of Southend on 29 March 1969. *(Essex Police Museum)*

In 1969 a report by a government Inspector recommended the amalgamation of Southend with the county force, and a combined police authority was established to oversee the proposed new force. The new force came into being on 1 April 1969. Pictured is the brochure for the final parade and salute, which took place on 29 March 1969. *(Essex Police Museum)*

Above: The distinctive DMW motorcycles used by the force taking part in the final parade. DMW was the last motorcycle manufacturer in Wolverhampton. The company, which closed in the mid-1990s, was also one of the longest running, having produced its first motorcycle about fifty years before its doors closed for the last time. *(Essex Police Museum)*

Left: The Essex Police Museum produced a booklet 'The Borough Men' to commemorate the history of the Southend Borough Constabulary and their proud history from 1914 until 1969. The booklet gives the names of all officers who served in the force during this time. *(Essex Police Museum)*

FOUR

ESSEX AND SOUTHEND-ON-SEA JOINT CONSTABULARY

1969–1974

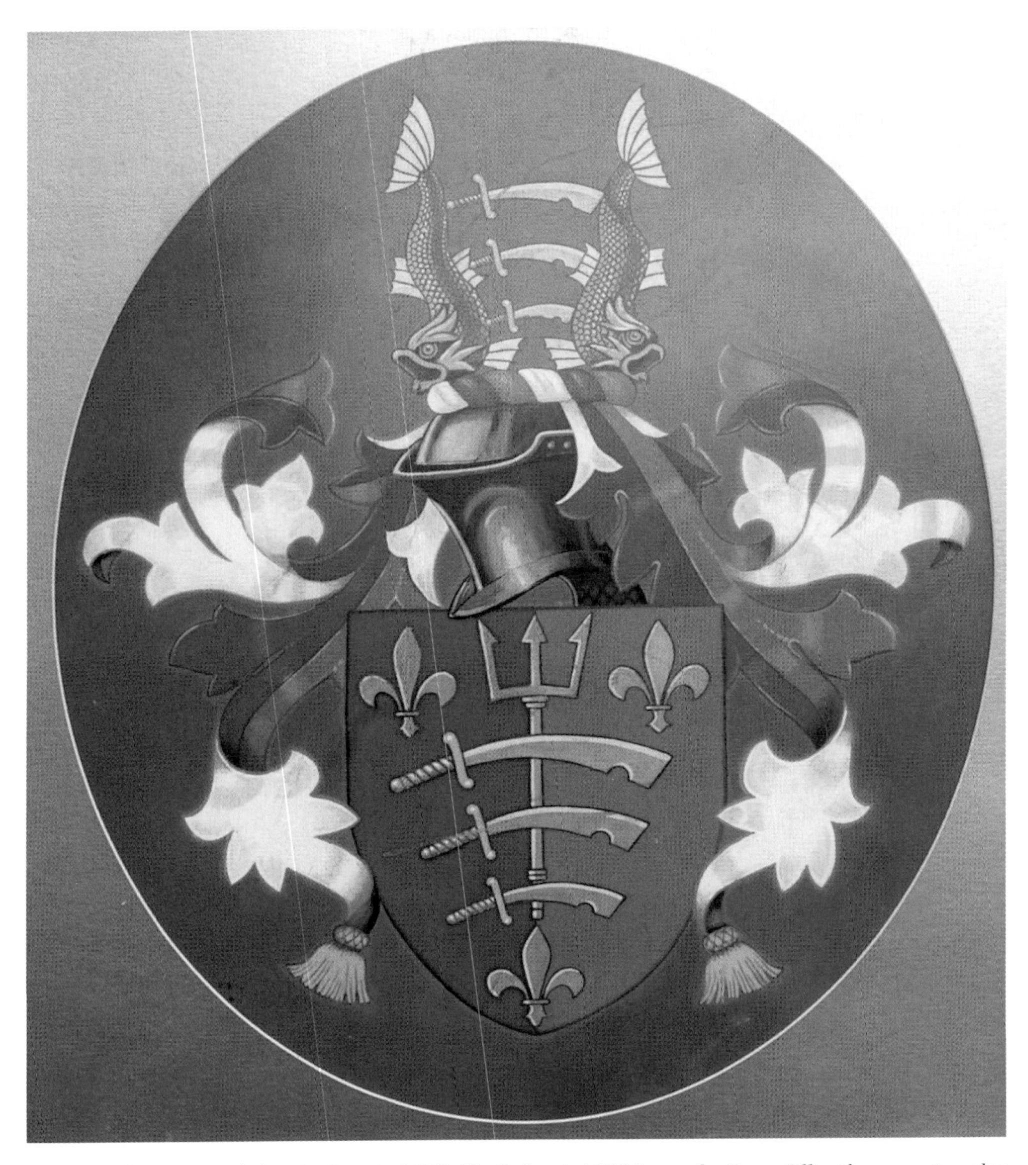

The Coat of Arms awarded to the force in 1970. The Police Act 1964 gave the Home Office the power to order compulsory amalgamations of forces. An attempt was made in 1966 to get Southend and Essex to amalgamate on a voluntary basis, but this was objected to by the Watch Committee. Following a public enquiry, the 1986 Government Inspector's Report recommended amalgamation. The new force came into being on 1 April 1969 and would be known as the Essex and Southend-on-Sea Joint Constabulary.

Sir John Nightingale, seen here seated in his office at headquarters, was appointed Chief Constable of the new force. The establishment of the joint force was 2,316 officers, although the actual strength at the end of year stood at 1,934.

ESSEX and SOUTHEND-on-SEA
JOINT CONSTABULARY

CHIEF CONSTABLE'S
ANNUAL REPORT
1969

ESSEX CONSTABULARY

SOUTHEND-ON-SEA CONSTABULARY

The Annual Report of 1969 for the new force.

Police cadets outside Police Headquarters in 1951. The first female cadets were not appointed until 1961. *(Essex Police Museum)*

The first intake at the newly opened Cadet School. The first commandant was Chief Inspector John Hedgethorne. The emphasis was on providing general education for cadets, with short attachments to police departments in the final months, before joining as police constables. The three-year course was residential. Full-time training for cadets ceased in 1978 and the Cadet School became the Force Training School. *(Essex Police Museum)*

HRH Princess Anne is accompanied by John Nightingale at the official opening of the Police Cadet School at Police Headquarters, on 20 October 1969. *(Essex Police Museum)*

Essex & Southend-on-Sea Joint Constabulary

POLICE CADET SCHOOL

OFFICIAL OPENING

by

Her Royal Highness The Princess Anne

on

Monday, 20th October, 1969

Above left: The recruiting booklet for the Police Cadets. *(Essex Police Museum)*

Above right: The official brochure for the opening of the Cadet School. *(Essex Police Museum)*

Left: The Essex Police Band was formed in 1966 when a group of musicians got together to perform an impromptu concert at a dinner at Police Headquarters, borrowing instruments from the Witham British Legion. Since those early days the band has gone from strength to strength and is in popular demand. It consists of serving officers and also support staff. *(Essex Police Museum)*

Abovee: Staff and vehicles of the Traffic Division based at Laindon, near Basildon. Under the command of a Chief Superintendent, the strength of the traffic division in 1971 stood at 177 officers of all ranks. They were based at various garages around the county. The vehicle fleet consisted of Ford Cortina GTs, Mini Cooper S, Vauxhall Victor, Triumph 2.5 PI cars, Ford Transit vans and Triumph and Norton motorcycles. *(Essex Police Museum)*

Left: PC Graham Collier, who joined in 1961, portrays an image that most people associate with policing in the 1970s and '80s. *(Essex Police Museum)*

Below: The Women Police Department had it own separate identity and own promotion structure, and by the end of 1973 the number of women officers in the force stood at ninety-six. Superintendent Welburn was the first female Superintendent in Essex. Appointed in 1970, she was responsible for preparing the women officers for the ending of the separate women's department in 1975. After 1975 women had equal pay and could start to train to do the same jobs as male officers. *(Essex Police Museum)*

Officers of the Women Police Department photographed in 1971. Superintendent Welburn is seated next to ACC Charles Waller. *(Essex Police Museum)*

Inspector Bob George and PC Ken Wright with a vehicle on permanent loan from the Police Research Centre based outside St Albans, Hertfordshire. It was used for rescuing people stuck in the treacherous mud flats off the Essex coast. *(Essex Police Museum)*

The vehicle workshops at Police Headquarters opened in August 1971. They remained in use until 2006, when they were transferred to a new location. *(Essex Police Museum)*

FIVE

ESSEX POLICE

1947 TO THE PRESENT DAY

The brief five-year history of the Essex and Southend-on-Sea Joint Constabulary came to an end on 1 April 1974 when it was succeeded by the Essex Police, which had precisely the same area of jurisdiction. All officers serving in the joint constabulary were transferred to the new force, which was still under the command of John Nightingale, who was to be knighted in 1975. With the formation of the new force came the introduction of navy and white diced cap bands. The strength of the force stood at 2,214 officers.

Sir John Nightingale retired in 1978 and was replaced as Chief Constable by Robert Sidney Bunyard (pictured). He was born in 1930, and saw service with the Metropolitan Police. He transferred to Essex as Deputy Chief Constable in 1977 from Leicestershire where he had been an Assistant Chief Constable. He took up his new post in July 1978 but resigned in December 1987 to take up the post of Commandant of the Police Staff College, Bramshill, with the rank of Her Majesty's Inspector of Constabulary. He was knighted in 1991. *(Essex Police Museum)*

A photograph taken at Police Headquarters shows the various departments of the force. In the front are the chief officers. From left to right: Peter Simpson, Ronald Stone, Robert Bunyard, Matt Comrie and John Challis. *(Essex Police Museum)*

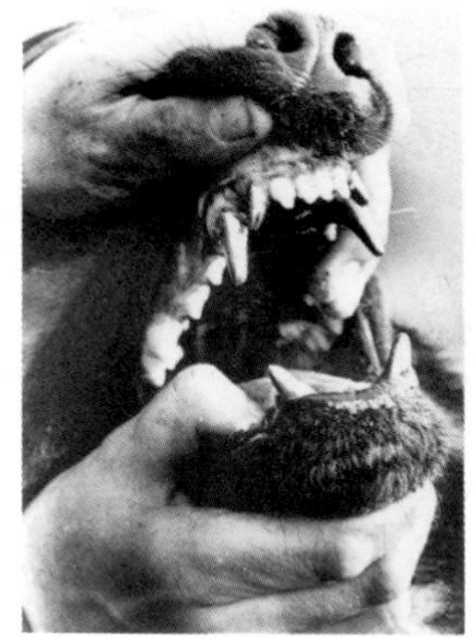

In 1979, three-year-old police dog, Bruce, made veterinary history when he was fitted with rust-proof, nickel-chromium canine teeth by surgeons at Bristol veterinary college, after he broke his own teeth while training. The success of the operation attracted a great deal of media interest. Bruce is seen here with his handler, PC Michael Mercer. *(Essex Police Museum)*

Sergeant Paul Hemmings on Cavalier. The Police Mounted Section was disbanded in 1999 as part of a cost cutting exercise, but was re-introduced in 2007 under the present Chief Constable. The section had a policy that the horses name had to start with the letter 'C'. *(Essex Police Museum)*

In 1984 the force was shocked at the murder of PC Brian 'Bill' Bishop, a firearms officer, who had served in Essex from 1966. He was shot by an armed criminal who had just carried out a robbery at a local bank at Frinton-on-Sea on 22 August. He died five days later in hospital from his injuries. *(Essex Police Museum)*

On 19 February 1986, the then Home Secretary, Douglas Hurd, unveiled a brown granite memorial stone adjacent to the seafront site where Bill Bishop fell. It was funded by the Police Memorial Trust. *(Essex Police Museum)*

John Halcrow Burrow became the eighth Chief Constable when he was appointed to the post on 1 February 1988. Born in 1935, he was commissioned into the 3rd Kenya Battalion, King's African Rifles, between 1953 and 1955. He joined the Metropolitan Police in 1958, becoming Assistant Chief Constable (1977) and Deputy Chief Constable of Merseyside (1983). He was national president of the Association of Chief Police Officers in 1992-93. He was appointed the CBE, and retired on 30 June 1998. He was to oversee the celebrations marking the 150th anniversary of the foundation of the force in 1990. *(Essex Police Museum)*

Service of Thanksgiving
to Celebrate
the 150th Anniversary
of the
Foundation of
Essex Police

Chelmsford Cathedral
Sunday, 23rd September 1990
at 4.00 p.m.

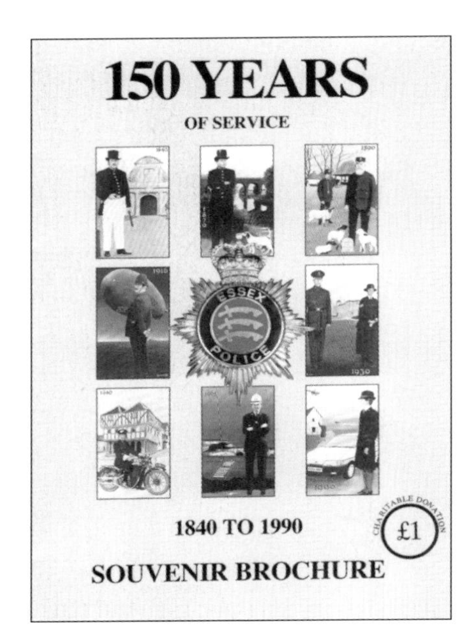

FOREST WATCH

SUMMER 1995

Published by Herts & Essex Newspapers on behalf of Epping, Ongar, North Weald and villages **Neighbourhood Watch Association**

Winning the fight to conquer crime

RECENTLY-released figures show that we are winning the battle against crime.

Although much has been written about the pros and cons of Neighbourhood Watch, local people have shown that if you want it to work and put enough effort into it, it will work.

Residents of North Weald and Thornwood have produced amazing figures for their efforts.

People living in a crime-hit, 350-house estate have helped reduce the burglary rate from one a month to one in 19 months. On another estate, in Thornwood, residents have reduced their high burglary rate to nil over a 10-month period.

Epping Round Table, North Weald village day committee and Thornwood residents' committee have assisted with money to purchase street signs for these groups.

Residents of Lower Sheering are the latest to join the battle — each resident on the estate has put hand into pocket to raise the cash.

Detection figures for the Epping and Ongar police area are way above the national average — Ongar's detection rate is above 50 per cent — and with the parishes of North Weald, Lavers and Sheering containing over 110 Neighbourhood Watch groups, the message goes out loud and clear: **Villains, watch out, you are being watched.**

● EYES OPEN: Teresa and Georgina Nickolson and PC Chris Caten with a Neighbourhood Watch street sign at Thornwood

Guv's on his home turf

WE extend a warm welcome to Inspector Peter Hesketh, *above*, the new governor for the Epping Ongar Police area.

Peter will be on familiar turf — he lives with his wife in High Ongar and, three years after joining the force in 1971, spent five years as a PC at Ongar Police Station.

Before that he had been at Harlow and, after another stint there when he became a sergeant, then divisional crime prevention officer, Peter moved to Stansted Airport. He was promoted to inspector and returned to Harlow four years ago.

Now based at Epping, Peter, who has two grown-up children, sees the challenge he faces as giving value for money without losing the traditional, personal touch of policing.

Above left: The order of service for the service of thanksgiving in Chelmsford Cathedral. *(Essex Police Museum)*

Above right: The souvenir booklet issued as part of the 150th celebrations. *(Essex Police Museum)*

Left: As part of the Neighbourhood Watch Programme in Essex, the then Epping and Ongar Sub-division, which was part of the Harlow Division, produced a regular newspaper called *Forest Watch*. *(Essex Police Museum)*

Below: The Chief Constable's cap. *(Essex Police Museum)*

Roger Baker became the tenth Chief Constable of Essex in 2005. He had joined Derbyshire Constabulary on 25 July 1977 and worked in various uniform CID and Command roles. In 2001 he was appointed as Assistant Chief Constable (Territorial Policing) and Assistant Chief Constable (Crime and Operations) in Staffordshire Police. In 2003 he was became a Deputy Chief Constable in North Yorkshire Police. He was given the Queens Police Medal (QPM) in 2008 and retired in July 2009. *(Essex Police Museum)*

Above: A map showing the current six divisions of the force. *(Essex Police Museum)*

Left: George Cook is the chief officer of the Special Constabulary. He started his career in Southend when he joined the Southend Borough Special Constabulary as Special Constable No. 613 on 3 December 1963. He can rightfully claim to be the only Southend officer still serving. He was awarded the MBE in 2003 for services to the police. *(Essex Police Museum)*

The importance of policing the coast around Essex has been recognised for many years, but it has taken on a new significance with the threat to this country through international terrorism. Here members of the Marine Unit demonstrate *Seaxe* and *Sentinel*, two Halmatic Arctic 24s launched in July 2005 and are based at Burnham on Crouch Marina. Each boat can take up to six officers and is capable of deploying for major incidents and firearms related jobs on the water. *(Essex Police Museum)*

Left and below: The Air Support Unit was formed in 1990, and Boreham Airfield, near Chelmsford, was chosen as the operating base. The initial establishment of the unit was an Inspector, a Sergeant and four police constables. The first helicopter was an Aerospatiale AS355 F1 Squirrel registered as G-XPOL. In 1998 a decision was taken to end the lease and to purchase the force's own helicopter. The aircraft chosen was an Aerospatiale AS355 F2 Squirrel registered as G-EPOL. *(Essex Police Museum)*

In 1999 Essex stopped using motorcycles as part of a £7m cost-cutting exercise. However their usefulness was recognised and in 2006 they were re-introduced into the force. *(Essex Police Museum)*

Great Dunmow police station opened in 2008 to replace the original station built in 1842. It cost £5 million to build and is used as a base for road policing, dogs and scenes of crime, among others. *(Martyn Lockwood)*

A decision was taken in 2006 to re-introduce a mounted section in the force. The first four horses were introduced in 2007 following training. The section is now based on the outskirts of Chelmsford and currently has eight horses. The tradition of naming horses with names beginning with the letter 'C' was abandoned and it was left to local children to choose the names. Pictured here are Sergeant Dave Martin on Bella (left) and PC Dale Copley on Biscuit. *(Essex Police Museum)*

Members of the Force Support Unit. *(Essex Police Museum)*

Jim Barker-McCardle was appointed Chief Constable on the retirement of Roger Baker, and took up his new post in September 2009. The photograph shows him shaking hands with Mr Robert Chambers, Chair of the Essex Police Authority, on his appointment. Mr Barker-McCardle joined Kent Police in 1981 and served throughout the county in both uniform and detective posts. Appointed Deputy Chief Constable in March 2004, he was involved in the early stages of the collaboration programme between Essex Police and Kent Police before transferring to the National Policing Improvement Agency in November 2007 as Deputy Chief Constable and Deputy Chief Executive. He was awarded the Queen's Police Medal in Her Majesty the Queen's 2007 birthday honours. *(Heather Turner)*

DCC Andy Bliss presenting medals to the Royal Military Police stationed at Colchester on their return from duty in Afghanistan. When back in Colchester, the RMP officers share the Garrison police station with officers from both Essex Police and the Ministry of Defence Police and they have built up a close relationship with their Essex Police counterparts. *(Essex Police Museum)*

Above and left: The memorials at Police Headquarters in memory of those officers of Colchester Borough, Southend Borough and Essex County Constabulary who paid the supreme sacrifice in two world wars. Their names will live on forever. *(Essex Police Museum)*

Other titles published by The History Press

A History of the Northamptonshire Police

RICHARD COWLEY

Illustrated with over 200 photographs, documents and ephemera, the majority of which have never before been published, *A History of the Northamptonshire Police* features images of policemen and women at work and at leisure, together with scene of crime photographs and mugshots of criminals between the 1870s and '80s, which, coupled with informative captions, offer a unique insight into the force's history.

978 0 7509 4956 9

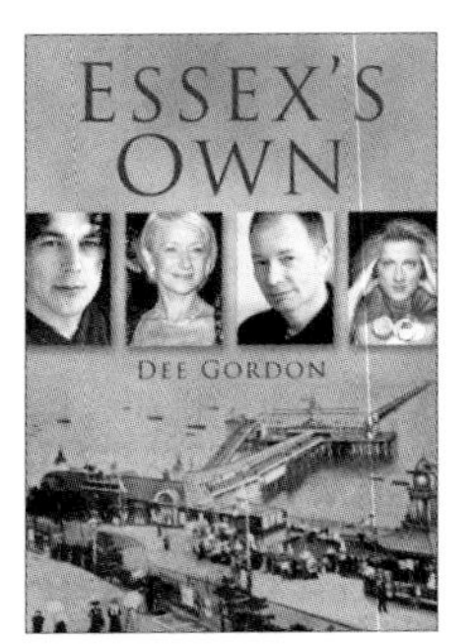

Essex's Own

DEE GORDON

Athlete and TV presenter Sally Gunnell, painter Edward Bawden, actress Joan Sims, singer Billy Bragg, footballer Bobby Moore, chef Jamie Oliver, author John Fowles, film director Basil Dearden, playwright Sarah Kane, and the infamous highwayman Dick Turpin are among personalities through the ages who have been born in Essex. This book features mini-biographies of all these and many more, and will make fascinating reading for residents and visitors alike.

978 0 7509 5121 0

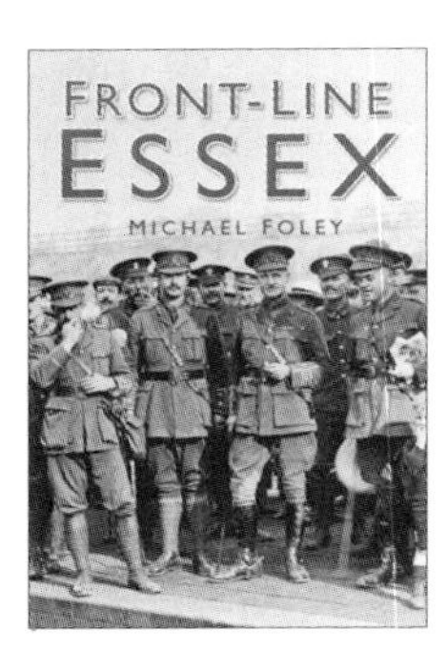

Front-Line Essex

MICHAEL FOLEY

Michael Foley's book delves into the long history of military Essex, from Harwich's redoubt fortress and associated Martello towers, built to keep Napoleon out, to the truth behind gunpowder at Purfleet and cavalry in Chelmsford, from Harwich's naval base, which saw the surrender of 122 German U-Boats at the end of the First World War, to the British and American Air Force bases throughout the county, not forgetting a Cold War bunker that is secret no longer.

978 0 7509 4260 7

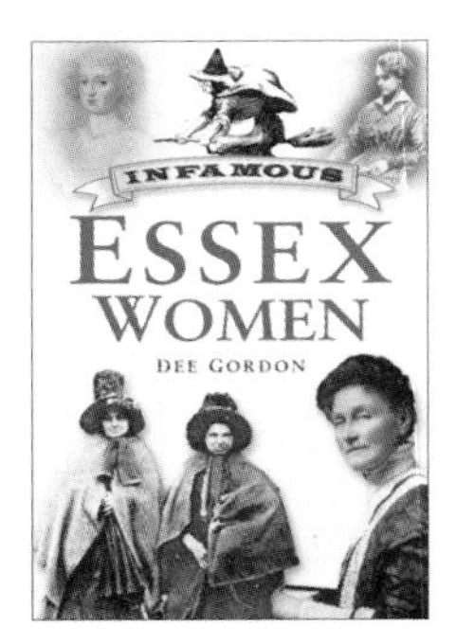

Infamous Essex Women

DEE GORDON

From the thirteenth century onwards, Essex has produced more than its fair share of infamous women. The reader will find a plethora of women to hate, ridicule or secretly admire in Dee Gordon's new book. Some of the characters featured here might horrify or mystify, others will provoke empathy or disbelief, but all tales are authenticated by hours of research. Read, learn, squirm – and smile!

978 0 7509 5085 5

Visit our website and discover thousands of other History Press books.